The Center for Discovery
P.O. Box 840
Harris, NY 12742
(Please write "Walter's Way on the memo
field of check)

P9-DEI-232

WALTER'S WAY

WALTER'S WAY

How a Relief Kid Survived TB, Corporate Betrayal, Bankruptcy,
Made Millions, and Touched the Lives of Billions

WALTER J. SCHERR

Published by John Wiley & Sons, Inc., Hoboken, New Jersey.
Published simultaneously in Canada.

For general information on our other products and services or for technical support, please contact our Customer Care Department within the United States at (800) 762-2974, outside the United States at (317) 572-3993 or fax (317) 572-4002.

Wiley publishes in a variety of print and electronic formats and by print-on-demand. Some material included with standard print versions of this book may not be included in e-books or in print-on-demand. If this book refers to media such as a CD or DVD that is not included in the version you purchased, you may download this material at http://booksupport.wiley.com. For more information about Wiley products, visit www.wiley.com.

ISBN 978-1-119-11843-5 (Hardcover)
Printed in the United States of America
10 9 8 7 6 5 4 3 2 1

Dedicated to the caretakers of the world.

A bucket list is mandatory when you get to be my age,

To finish things so long put off so I can turn the page.

I took my time, I wrote my list, peace I hoped to find,

So I can leave this place called Earth with a clearer mind.

Atop my list at number one was a visit to the beaches of D-Day,

To pay my respects to the young heroes who bravely led the way.

To understand at last, dear God, why it was not me,

Who died beneath those tall white cliffs that day in Normandy.

—Walter Scherr

DISCLAIMER

The events in this book are portrayed to the best of Walter J. Scherr's memory. However, since memories can be flawed, there may be errors. Also, in order to protect the privacy of people involved, some names and identifying details have been changed. Some of the timelines have been compressed to avoid confusing the readers; and some of the dialogue and conversations have been re-created to the best of Mr. Scherr's recollections of events long past.

SAVING PRIVATE BOWEN

ON THE RAIN-SWEPT BLUFFS OVERLOOKING OMAHA BEACH, I WEPT BEFORE the grave of a man I had never met.

It was October 2014—and at the age of 90 I had finally made my way to the hallowed ground of the American Cemetery at Normandy: The final resting place for 9,387 souls, most of whom lost their lives in the fighting of June 1944 and the months that followed.

These young men—men of my generation—died in the fight against fascism.

It was a fight I had longed so desperately to be a part of.

Now I was here to pay my respects to them—and to one in particular. My wife Sylvia and I had traveled to France, enjoying a boat cruise down the Seine en route to Normandy. Although I had not landed here in 1944 with a rifle in my hands, I had visited France many times in the decades to follow. I had done business here, and made friends—a few of whom I was delighted to see during the 10-day trip through the scenic French countryside.

Still, the culmination—the main purpose, really—was to come to Normandy. It wasn't easy—international travel is difficult for most people of my age; and particularly as I must use a wheelchair for anything more arduous than walking around the house.

So why make this difficult journey, when I could have, say, visited the National World War II Museum in New Orleans? Or said a prayer in church on Memorial Day? Or simply re-watched the famous D-Day movies *Saving Private Ryan* or *The Longest Day* again in the comfort of my living room?

Because in my opinion this is a place every American should visit to understand the significance of what happened here; and the sacrifices made.

For me, though, it was something more.

I had carried with me to France a piece of paper with a name and a few sentences scribbled on it. Information we'd found from online service records:

Bowen, Francis N.
Private
508th Parachute Infantry Regiment
Date of Death: June 15, 1944
Buried: Plot E Row 13 Grave 6 Normandy American Cemetery
Colleville-sur-Mer, France
Awards: Purple Heart

Bowen was born in 1921—three years before me. He grew up in the New York City borough of Queens, same as me. According to his enlistment records, he was 5-feet, 10-inches tall, and weighed 123 pounds. A string bean, much as I had been at his age.

I had found Bowen's name while searching D-Day veterans from Queens. I never knew him personally, but he could have easily been one of my pals. He was probably like a lot of the guys I grew up with in the Queens community of Ozone Park—many of whom, like Bowen, did march off to war in late 1941 and 1942. His friends probably called him Fran, Frank, or Franny; he would have been a kid during the Great Depression, and perhaps like me, could very well have known the anxiety of having a father out of work (I did—and given that the unemployment rate during the depths of the Depression was nearly 25 percent, so did many). As a kid, Francis Bowen probably tried to help out as best he could: delivering papers, collecting bottle caps for the deposit money. He probably attended church dutifully on Sundays (most of us did in those days, whether you liked it or not); played stickball in the streets; and on hot summer nights, escaped his crowded little Queens house to sit on the stoop, watching the world go by.

As a teenager, he might have very well frequented the same ice cream parlors, the same movie theaters on Liberty Avenue, a main shopping thoroughfare in that part of Queens. Maybe like me, he was even listening to the Giants game on the radio in December 1941, as I was when news came over of the Japanese attack on Pearl Harbor.

Yes, in a manner of speaking, I felt I really knew Francis Bowen, even though we had never met.

And in the back of my mind, the refrain that had echoed—now more loudly than ever—at many points in my life; the realization that is part of what drove me here in the twilight of my life, to visit a young man who had been cut down in the prime of his life.

This could have been me.

Why did I survive ... why was I given the opportunity to live the life and do the things I'd done, while he never lived beyond his 23rd birthday?

Bowen was killed nine days after the landings of June 6, in the long, bloody fighting that ensued for the next two months amidst the hedgerows, farms, and villages of Normandy's Cotentin Peninsula. The night before our ship was to dock at Normandy, I woke up in the middle of the night. Now that I had finally arrived, I was anxious and needed to clarify, in my own mind at least, what had compelled me to come all this way. I tried to put some of my thoughts about this in the form of a poem. I'm no Frost or Eliot, but while my initials aren't T.S. there was no B.S. in what I tried to express in my words. They were about my need to pay homage to Bowen and his comrades; about my search for some kind of answer to the question of why-them-and-not-me; about why I was on a cruise ship enjoying my golden years, and they were buried in the French soil.

I then knelt on the deck of the ship and prayed. I asked God for something that I suspect is unusual in petitions to Him: lousy weather. So far, it had been sunny, crisp fall days in our trip to France. But I didn't want that for Normandy. I wanted it to be the way it was at the time of D-Day when a system of storms and gale force winds had threatened to halt the entire operation. I told God that I wanted this so that I could be there in spirit with the boys.

God must have heard me. Indeed, I suspect he must have thought: "This guy wants bad weather? I'll give him weather he'll never forget."

The next morning, a gale had blown up on the English Channel. The winds were fierce, the rain blowing sideways. It was far worse than on the morning of June 6, in fact, but more like the miserable day prior to the landings, which the invasion forces had spent waiting, most of them seasick, in their armada of transport ships.

That wasn't likely to happen to us on a securely docked, 21st century cruise ship. Still, the conditions were so treacherous there was fear that some of the older folks on our cruise wouldn't even be able to get down the gangplank.

Luckily, I had made a new friend during our holiday and, like so many of my dear friends, he came through for me. Calvin, the strapping, former security head for NASA, had flown a helicopter in Vietnam, and now runs a mission feeding hungry people in Florida. He was a Godly man, and what we used to call a "man's man." Calvin was accompanied on his trip by his wife, Jan. The four of us—Calvin, Jan, Sylvia, and I—had met and become fast friends. We had much in common in terms of our tastes and values. But Calvin was younger than me and considerably larger and stronger, as well. He knew of my desire to visit the cemetery and find Bowen's grave, and so he took matters into his own hands. Literally: As I hovered near the gangplank in my wheelchair, the crew debating whether it was safe for me to disembark, Calvin simply bent down, lifted me into his muscular arms and carried me like a child to shore.

The American Cemetery is usually crowded with visitors and buses. Not this day, as the rain had kept many away. A small group of us took the tour and listened to our French guide pay homage to the Americans.

My heart stirred with patriotic pride at his words. "Thank God for these men," said the guide, a young Frenchman, gesturing towards the expanse of white crosses. "Without them, I wouldn't have been here. The Germans surely would have killed my parents and grandparents."

Mindful of the conditions, he gave us an abbreviated tour of the beautiful 172-acre national cemetery, which was officially opened in 1956.

At the end, we were told that anyone who wanted to visit a grave should do so now. The rest of our group was eager to get back on the ship, but I was on a mission. The four of us, following directions we had been given, made our way to the site of what we were told was Bowen's grave. It was slow going. They were repairing some of the walkways, the ground was muddy and there were construction materials piled up here and there. At each barrier, we'd stop and Calvin would pick me up as Sylvia pushed my empty chair. Then he'd gently place me back down.

Finally we came to the designated spot. We checked the number: This was it. But to my disappointment, we were looking at what appeared to be a blank, white cross. We cast quizzical glances at each other and shrugged. "I guess this is it," I said. And then I took the poem out of my pocket and began to read it aloud.

I had barely begun when a woman appeared out of nowhere. She was thin, of medium height, and wore a blue raincoat and had a white scarf covering head, so that you could hardly see her face.

"Are you trying to see the name?" she asked in heavily accented English.

"Oui, yes," we said.

"You need one of these!" she said, holding up what appeared to be a little cup filled with sand.

She handed it to me. "Like so," she said, pantomiming a rubbing motion across the center of the granite cross. I rolled up close to the headstone, and rubbed it with the moistened sand, which I later learned came from Omaha Beach, below the bluffs the cemetery was built on. The principle is that the wet sand fills in the carvings of the grave for better visibility. But the effect is startling: if this were a movie, you would have heard at this point the music swelling or an angelic chorus, because almost as if by magic, there appeared the name carved on the cross.

Francis N. Bowen

I was shaking—from either the cold rain or the power of the moment. It was if he had appeared; awoken from eternal sleep to acknowledge our presence.

I finished the poem and said a few words in silence to Bowen.

"I've come a long way to see you," I intoned, as tears streamed down my face. "I know we never met, but I feel like we did. And I want you to know that I would have been here too if I could have been. But I've tried to live a life worthy of your sacrifice."

I turned around to thank the woman who gave me the sand. She was gone. The others craned their necks looking for her as well. The cemetery is a wide open place, and yet she had seemingly vanished. "Where the heck could she have gone?" Calvin wondered.

A Mystery Lady, I thought to myself, and, amidst the tears, actually had to suppress a chuckle. She wasn't the first one in my life.

I turned back to Bowen's cross. The words were again illegible as the rain pelted us. I sat and stared momentarily, thinking about him, thinking about his sacrifice and about my life. Sylvia leaned down, and whispered gently, "Walter, it's time to go."

***

WALTER'S WAY

Sylvia was right. My mission was accomplished. In a larger sense, I realize the truth of those words. At 90 years old, it is almost time to go. But I intend to leave something behind.

That brings us to the book you are now holding in your hands. You may be wondering about why I wrote this book and its title: Who is this Walter guy, and why should I care about his "way"?

I'm Walter J. Scherr, and let me assure you, that "way" in the title is not as in, "my way or the highway." It's about how I've made my way...unsure, often; stumbling, even falling flat on my face a few times ... through a life that has had its ups and downs; trials and triumphs.

When you get to be my age, people assume you must have some kind of secret formula for longevity. I am asked often about the "secret" of life. My answer, in three words: life goes on.

While our time on Earth is rounded with a peaceful sleep, no one really dies as long as there is one person in the living world who remembers him or her, remembers their words, or shares their thoughts with others. All who have lived and have been loved have earned a piece of immortality.

I believe that and I believe this as well. It's what I tell when I'm asked another question. This one I get a lot, too, particularly from my grandchildren, who are now beginning to making their way into adult life.

"What do you need to be happy?"

Here again, I answer not with a shrug, or a sigh or some vague "it depends" response. No, sir: I know what it takes to achieve happiness, at least for me.

First, a moral code to follow.

Second, a cause to serve.

Third, a goal to believe in.

And for me, all those have converged here. My code, my cause, my goal...and hopefully my legacy, as well...are all here in these pages, which relate the story of my life and the lessons learned.

While I would never compare what I endured to the murderous fire Francis Bowen and his comrades faced in Normandy—or any combat, for that matter—I can tell you that I went through a hell of my own for nearly eight years; twice the length of our involvement in World War II. I can also tell you that I came from nothing (nothing that is, aside from a loving family and a solid network of friends, pillars upon which my life still rests).

In *Walter's Way*, you'll find many adventures and excitement as well as disappointment and heartache. You'll see that I traveled over two million miles and to 40 countries over the course of my career as a corporate executive and entrepreneur. I helped introduce the fax machine to North America; I was a founding board member of four international corporations, including one that was a pioneer in data storage—a precursor to today's Cloud. Although I must admit I still need my grandkids to help me program my cell phone, I am proud to say I was one of the pioneers in what would later become, in various manifestations, the "high-tech" industry.

I also produced a Hollywood film, worked in the defense industry, and helped my two sons establish an oil and gas exploration company.

My varied enterprises have on occasion been deemed newsworthy, as I have been profiled in both *Fortune* and the *Wall Street Journal* as well as *Newsday*, the newspaper serving the vast New York suburb of Long Island, where I have lived for most of my adult life.

But my story is anything but a smooth rise to the top: At one point in my career, I was blindsided and almost left destitute by one of the world's largest international companies. I almost lost my home; I watched my bank account plummet from full to empty in a frighteningly fast time. I even spent a brief time in detention in a Communist country.

For reasons you'll read about in the next few chapters, I really didn't even begin my career until I was in my late 20s. Maybe that's why I was so driven to succeed. I always felt like I had a lot of catching up to do with my peers, who were already out of college and ensconced in their businesses by that point.

"That point" was the late 1940s—ancient history to most people alive today. If you've watched shows like *Madmen* or movies like *Unbroken*, you may wonder about what life was really like in those "distant" decades of the 20th century.

By all means read on, because I was there for it all: I had a bird's-eye view of the Cold War, as I worked for a couple of this country's major defense contractors when our stand-off with the Russians was at its frostiest. But, a decade later, in the mid-1960s, I visited and embraced the culture of India, like the Beatles (although maybe not quite in the same way they did). I watched the economic juggernaut of post-war America reach full steam in the 1960s; and would probably have been considered a part of what was then called the "jet set" simply because I seemed to spend so much time in the air—flying all over the globe to close a deal, put out a fire, or exploit a new business opportunity.

In 1970, I became part of what would eventually be called the high-tech industry, helping to pioneer the introduction to businesses of what was then a remarkable innovation: The fax machine.

In the 1980s, I was involved with video and film (imagine, me, a Relief kid from Queens whose first real job was as a junior accountant ... in Hollywood!).

In the 1990s, I continued my involvement in the rising tide of the technology industry, working with companies that produced data storage systems, LEDs, and atomic-force microscopes.

I'm also here to tell you that it's never too late to build a successful company, or as they like to say today, "reinvent" yourself. At the age of 66, I started a new business with a group of fellow, like-minded entrepreneurs. Our first year, 1991, we had $31 million in debt, and $25 million in sales. The balance sheet showed 5 times more debt than equity. Fifteen years later the company was valued at one billion dollars!

Over the years, my work often took me to such "hip" locales as New York City's SoHo section and Beverly Hills, and to what was then called "Swinging London" in the 1960s (although I must confess, even at age 36, I was a bit too old to be one of the swingers at that point).

Yet, despite my trips to cool and exotic places, I was also a conventional suburban guy with a beautiful wife and four wonderful kids.

I love my family—which now includes grandchildren and even great grandchildren!—I love my country, and I still go to church every Sunday.

Does that sound boring? I hope not, because along Walter's Way, I have met some very memorable characters, including a sprinkling of celebrities and major world figures; and I have found myself in some tricky, hilarious, outrageous, and occasionally dangerous situations.

I have also learned a thing or two about business, about success, and about life (hey, when you've reach my age, you better have learned a few things, right?). For example: I have discovered that if you combine an old math formula and an egg, you can produce extraordinary results in both your professional and personal life. While this isn't a how-to book per se, I will explain that to you; and impart a few of the other principles I've learned, not only from my successes, but from the failures as well.

In fact, if you're someone right now who is going through a tough spot in your life, personally or professionally, I particularly hope you will turn these pages to find some inspiration—or at least to see that others have been there as well. I'm here to tell you that you shouldn't quit; it can, it will get better if you want it to.

While I did make money through my various endeavors, I have spent the last decade trying to give a lot of it away. Which brings me to the underlying purpose of the book.

Through every up and down of my life, I had a caretaker who helped me through, whether it was via advice, encouragement, medical care, or by simply giving me a chance. During the lowest point of my life, my caretakers were people with their own problems; people who would have been considered down and out themselves—and yet they kept me and many others alive.

Twenty years later, while in India, I attended a meeting with Mother Teresa (yes, *the* Mother Teresa—I told you I met some famous people!) in which she urged us to honor the caretakers. I felt that night like she was speaking directly to me, a person who was alive because of people like her and those who shared her ministry.

This book, in a sense, is a fulfillment of that calling: It is written to help support places where caretakers are doing their indispensable work every day. After all, the measure of who we are as a society lies in how we care for our most vulnerable citizens.

My work on behalf of these people has been ongoing. I am proud to say that I have sponsored scholarship programs for caretakers, supported respiratory therapy programs, and sponsored a comprehensive children's care center. This book is a launch pad for a new program I have created with my family foundation, designed to honor and create opportunities for such caretakers around the world. In fact, every penny earned from this book will go to this new initiative, which will represent a new model of individualized, comprehensive care and specialized treatment for special needs children.

You can read more about the particulars of my program at the end of this book.

But first, I'd like to invite you to turn the page; to allow me to tell you the story of a kid from Queens who, at an epic moment in both his life and the history of this country, found himself hurled into a new and frightening direction.

It was the beginning of a long journey; one that in a sense reached closure in the bluffs overlooking Omaha Beach, many years later.

What happened in between is my life. So won't you join me, as we follow Walter's Way?

WALTER'S WAY

WALTER'S WAR

I WAS A SEVENTEEN-YEAR-OLD BOY ON DECEMBER 7, 1941, A MILD WINTER day with gray, cloudy skies. I was on my porch in Ozone Park, New York, listening to the radio broadcast of the New York Giants football team play the Brooklyn Dodgers at the Polo Grounds (yes, there was once a now-defunct Brooklyn Dodgers football team, in addition to the now-departed Brooklyn Dodgers baseball team). It was a special day, because before the game started, the fans had paid tribute to Tuffy Leemans, the Giants' star running back. The final game of the regular season started at 2 o'clock, but at 2:26, the broadcaster suddenly broke off his commentary, and another voice came on. I still remember how annoyed I felt when I heard the following words: "From the United Press..." I started yelling at the radio, because no matter what the reason, no one interrupted the Giants game! I got quiet in a hurry when I stopped ranting long enough to listen to what the announcer was saying.

"We interrupt this broadcast to bring you this important bulletin from the United Press. Washington: The White House announces that the Japanese have attacked Pearl Harbor."

I flipped to another station where I heard a more detailed description of the Japanese bombing of the American naval base in Hawaii, in what amounted to a declaration of war against the United States. I later learned that at the Polo Grounds any servicemen in attendance were told over the public address system that they had to report immediately to their units. The game went on, and the Dodgers stunned the crowd by routing the Giants by a score of 21 to 7. But it no longer seemed important, because in what felt like a matter of minutes, everything had changed. Our country was at war.

My friends and I were ready to sign up and fight—the Japanese or the Germans, we didn't care. But my parents wanted me to graduate from high school, and I couldn't legally join the Army until I turned 18, a long six months away. In my close-knit Queens neighborhood, an American flag now hung from every house. None of us wanted to wait to be drafted, and my parents totally supported my decision to enlist. Every healthy young man was expected to join the military, and we were willing and proud to do so.

After graduation, instead of going out to look for a job as I would have during peacetime, my friends and I headed down to Whitehall Street in Manhattan, the main enlistment office for New York. I remember how we all gathered under the roaring El—the elevated train that ran over Liberty Avenue in Queens—talking about how we would become daring fighting pilots, gung-ho Marines, and heroic soldiers and sailors. We were excited and happy, joking with one another as we waited in line in Manhattan to fill out the paperwork. After completing all the forms, there was yet another long line, while we waited for the physical exams. The doctors poked and prodded, told us to bend over and touch the floor, ordered us to make a fist while our blood was drawn. They checked us for flat feet and told us to say "ahh" while they looked down our throats. They listened to our hearts with their stethoscopes and thumped our chests and told us to cough. We were tested for every possible mental and physical disease to ensure that we were healthy enough to kill Germans and Japanese.

I was feeling very confident about my future in the military, imagining my heroic deeds, and envisioning myself returning to the neighborhood with a chest full of medals. That is, until one of the doctors emerged from behind a curtained-off room. The look on his face was my first indication that something was wrong. I didn't yet understand that my life was about to come to a crashing halt. I wanted to believe that his expression was the result of too many long hours spent day after day testing eager young men about to go off to war. He gestured to me to join him behind the curtain and pronounced four words that instantly changed the entire course of my future. "You have active tuberculosis."

My blank look told him I had no idea what he was talking about. "Ac-tive tu-berc-u-losis," he repeated, emphasizing each syllable. I shrugged, as if he'd just told me I had acne or the chills, or some minor diagnosis that could be cured with a couple of pills. I didn't understand that I had just experienced the turning point—and defining moment—of my life to that point. He very quickly explained that TB was an often fatal disease that starts in the lungs and that the cure was complete bed rest.

"For how long?" I asked.

"A year, two years, sometimes longer."

"But when can I join the Army?"

The doctor still had a big crowd of men waiting to be examined. "Young man," he said sternly. "You are highly contagious. You can't join the Army, the Navy, or any other branch of the military. The only place you're going is to bed in a sanitarium where you'll be quarantined until you don't show any more signs of TB."

Reeling over this news, I hurriedly said goodbye to my buddies and dragged myself out of the center, away from what was supposed to be my future. I had been diagnosed with a potentially deadly disease, but I was too angry and full of self-pity to accept the diagnosis. My world had just collapsed; all my plans and expectations were shattered. I desperately needed to blame someone...anyone...including the people I loved most: my mother, my father, my siblings. Not even God was exempt from my fury.

Still in denial, I mentally reviewed the symptoms of TB and decided that the doctor had to be wrong. I couldn't remember the last time I'd had a cough bad enough to keep me home from school or work, and I definitely hadn't ever coughed up any blood. I felt exhausted most days, as if I were dragging a heavy load on my shoulders, but I had an almost full-time job at an A&P grocery store. I worked there after school on Monday through Friday from one in the afternoon until seven or eight o'clock. On Saturdays, the hours were even longer: I typically started at eight in the morning and didn't get home until nine or ten o'clock.

I spent most of those hours lugging crates of fruits and vegetables from the basement to the main floor. The building didn't have an elevator or an escalator, so I had to walk up and down the stairs many times a day. If there was an easier or efficient way to carry the cumbersome wooden crates, nobody bothered telling me about it. My muscles constantly ached from both the exertion and the dampness in the basement, and on Sundays I was often so exhausted that I couldn't drag myself out of bed to go to Mass. But the effort far outweighed the pain. I was not only bringing home money, but sometimes I could buy leftover fruits and vegetables for just a few pennies. The look on my mother's face made me forget how tired I was, and I felt so happy to contribute to our family's income.

So now I was being told I couldn't join the service...why? Because I was tired? Given that kind of grueling manual labor, who wouldn't be tired? As far as I could tell, considering that so many people I knew worked in similar jobs, everyone was tired!

I estimated I was working about 40 hours a week, six days a week at the A&P, on top of a full day of school. I was achy, with almost flu-like symptoms, but hadn't paid this much mind. I later learned that a significant percentage of those who had TB had pleurisy first. I never realized that—and, looking back, I believe it's what caused my TB.

Following Army orders, the doctor had sent my name to the public health department. I couldn't become a soldier, but now I, too, had to follow orders. Orders I didn't like. I was told that I must find a sanitarium where I would be quarantined.

As I skulked back to my neighborhood, I imagined people staring at me on the street and whispering to each other, "Stay away from him, he has TB." I don't remember whether I took my time or hurried home to break the news to my parents. In fact, my recollections of the next few weeks are lost in a blur of emotions, all of them negative. I had to stay behind while all the guys I knew from the neighborhood were getting shipped out to protect our country. It's no wonder I shut down and blocked out all but the most important details. No words could capture the pain I was feeling.

I've also blocked out the memory of my parents' reaction to my news, but I'm sure that they did what they could to be loving and supportive. We had no money to consult a private doctor, so I went to a public health facility where a second examination confirmed that, yes, I had active tuberculosis. But then came yet another shock. Because of the war, there were no empty beds in any of the facilities designated as public sanitariums. My only option was to be quarantined at home in my own bed, with my mother to take care of me!

So began "Walter's War." While the rest of the world was in turmoil thousands of miles away, while America was mobilizing for what would later be called our Great Crusade against fascism, I lay in bed and waged my own inner battle. I was tormented by confusion and fear, bitterness and anger. I knew the statistics for tuberculosis. The odds of survival were not in my favor. Shame and hopelessness became my closest companions. Someone had to be held accountable for this: I blamed my parents, yelled at them and demanded answers. "Why didn't you take better care of me? Why did you make me work so hard?" When they didn't respond—because what could they say?—I blamed God. "How could You let this happen to me? Why me?" I reminded Him of all I'd done, how faithful I had been, how well I had served the church: "I was an altar boy, I said the Rosary, and I went to confession!"

God answered me with silence.

I was a young man who was probably going to die in my own bed at home, while my friends and so many others were risking their lives for the sake of our country's freedom. Nobody gave a damn about me, and why should they? And even if I did somehow survive my personal hell, how would I live? How would I support myself? I would be someone to be avoided and ignored. I thought of myself in the worst possible terms: coward, worthless, a disappointment, outcast, pariah.

Each day felt like hell. The public health doctor had warned me again about how contagious I was, so my father and sisters weren't allowed anywhere near me. I had nobody to talk to except my mother, who brought me my meals, changed my sheets, and took care of me as if I were a small child. She never once complained, even though I alternated between lashing out at her and feeling overwhelmed by guilt for blaming her.

The only reason I was allowed out of bed was to use the bathroom, and then it was right back to bed again. At first, I spent a lot of time sleeping. I'm sure this was partly because of depression, but it was probably the effects of the TB, as well. There was no doubt that despite my feelings otherwise, I was indeed sick. Freed from my routine of school and work, I finally gave in to the deep fatigue that was actually a symptom of my illness. I didn't have much else to keep my mind busy. As the months passed and the Board of Health continued to look for an opening for me at a facility, I began to write my obituary, my eulogy, and the epitaph for my tombstone.

"Here lies Walter J. Scherr.

He stayed in bed and had his mother take care of him, while his friends defended the Free World."

The days were long and tedious and lonely. I read the sports pages, and I listened to news of the war on the radio, wondering where my pals were, where I would have been if I weren't imprisoned in my sick bed. I relied on two very entertaining diversions to break up my days: comedian Morey Amsterdam and the "Mystery Lady across the street."

Then only 16 years old and nicknamed the "Human Joke Machine" because he could make up a joke on demand about any topic, at age sixteen Amsterdam (who would later become known to TV audiences as Buddy on *The Dick Van Dyke Show*) was already cracking up audiences at one of Al Capone's Chicago speakeasies. He claimed to have left Chicago for Los Angeles after he got caught in the middle of a shootout at the club between two rival gangs. It was a great career move, because he was quickly hired by some of Hollywood's most famous performers. I listened to Morey Amsterdam on the radio, telling jokes, every morning from 9 until 1. As far as I was concerned, and I haven't changed my mind in over seventy years, he was the funniest comedian I've ever heard. I never missed a show, and I couldn't have, even if I had wanted to. Where else did I have to go? His jokes didn't cure me of tuberculosis, but they certainly took me out of my depression and gave me "a merry heart," at least for a few hours every day.

My other daily source of entertainment was provided by the Mystery Lady who lived across the street from me. I'd never met her and didn't know her real name, but after my mother, she became the second most important woman in my life at the time. I had a picture-perfect view of her through my bedroom window, which faced hers—and she never bothered to draw the blinds or close her curtains. At 10:05 every morning, I was treated to what seemed like a carefully choreographed show created especially for my viewing enjoyment.

She always began by taking off her bathrobe, which immediately grabbed my attention. Underneath the bathrobe, she wore a sheer white nightgown—another attention grabber, and the most provocative piece of clothing I'd ever seen on a woman. The first time I noticed her I wondered whether my fever had spiked so high that I was hallucinating! But I knew she was the real deal. I reveled in her performance every morning—and her routine inevitably got the better of me. Dressed only in her nightgown, which left nothing to my imagination, Mystery Lady always sat down at her vanity table and slowly combed her long brown hair. And then, the moment I waited for from one day to the next—she would remove her nightgown. Totally naked, she would reveal herself to me...the climax of the show! Because of how our windows were placed, I couldn't see anything below her shoulders. But that still left plenty to my developing imagination. And boy did my imagination take me to places I never knew existed!

I will always be grateful to the Mystery Lady for helping me through those long, dismal days of isolation. The strange thing is that I never got another glimpse of her after I returned years later from the tuberculosis sanitarium where I was eventually placed. I know I didn't imagine her, but I never learned who she was or where she ended up after the war. Or whether she really knew she was putting herself on display for one bedridden—and thoroughly appreciative—teenage boy.

WELFARE ISLAND

After five months of being confined to my bedroom, the Board of Health finally found room for me at a hospital for the chronically ill on Welfare Island. It was located on the East River between Manhattan and Queens—surrounded by water to keep the patients away from the rest of the city. Although what I really needed was a tuberculosis sanitarium where I could receive proper treatment, this move felt like the first step in my recovery. My family and I prayed that I would return home soon, totally cured, perhaps well enough to join the Army. Until the ambulance arrived to take me to the hospital, I hadn't realized how much I would miss my parents.

I had apologized to both of them, especially my mother, many times over, for making them the targets of my anger. She had never complained or made me feel like a burden, although I knew that taking care of me had put a tremendous strain on her time and energy. We were all crying as I waved goodbye from the back of the ambulance. My last sight before the driver slammed the doors shut was of my mother, blowing me kisses as tears ran down her cheeks. I never felt as alone as I did during what seemed like an endless ride in the back of that ambulance.

My situation didn't improve very much after I arrived at Welfare Island. Years later it would be re-christened Roosevelt Island, and is now the site of a vibrant, residential community. That wasn't the case in the 1940s. I was deposited at the entrance to a spooky-looking building, probably dating back from the 19th century, when this place—then known as Blackwell's Island—was the dumping ground for New York's City's infirm and unwanted. A few muted rays of light penetrating through dim, murky windows; I could hear the sounds of coughing, moaning, suffering. Long rows of cots, lines of bodies laying in stretchers waiting in a triage unit.

I was assigned to an ice-cold room with hundreds of other patients, all of us lying in row after row of beds. Many were simply waiting to die.

I was confined to bed because I was coughing up blood, and my sputum, checked daily by an orderly, showed that I still had active tuberculosis. Very few doctors worked on Welfare Island—most of them were off caring for servicemen—but I felt a kinship with the staff members who took care of us. We formed a friendship of sorts, probably because we were all social outcasts. They were mostly down-on-their-luck people who had been rejected by the military for various reasons. But they seemed not to mind that they ran the risk of being infected with the TB bacteria, maybe because they were grateful to have a bed to sleep in and three meals a day.

Every day was the same: long and tedious. I desperately missed my mother's loving attention, Morey Amsterdam's jokes, and the Mystery Lady's show. Once in a while, we'd receive a box of second-hand books, so I'd choose something and try to read it. But my attention span was limited, and lying flat on my back made reading more of a chore than a distraction.

I spent a lot of time sleeping, but then I'd wake up and feel overwhelmed by loneliness. Rather than give in to my despair, I spent many otherwise empty hours thinking about happier times with my family and friends.

My three younger sisters and I grew up in Ozone Park, located in south-central Queens, one of New York City's five boroughs. Most of Queens in the 1930s, and especially Ozone Park, were working-class communities, inhabited by first-and-second-generation immigrant families. Yet, despite their different backgrounds, everyone seemed to get along here, whether they were Italian, Irish, or Jewish. Without televisions or any of the electronic devices we take for granted today, we listened to the radio, read the paper, and provided our own entertainment.

Stickball, which we played on the street, was one of our favorite games. Each block had a stickball team, and we competed fiercely against one another. Home plate was in the middle of the street, and second base was in a straight line from it. To get to first base, we'd run to a parked car. Another parked car on the other side of the street served as third base. None of us could afford to buy sports equipment, so we used an old broomstick as our bat and a cheap ball similar to a tennis ball. We judged our opponent's batting ability by how many "sewers" he could hit—meaning how far his ball could travel between manhole covers. When someone stepped up to the plate, the players on the other team would yell to the outfielder: "He hits three sewers!" (Supposedly, when Willie Mays was a baseball star for the 1950s New York Giants, he'd play a day game at the Polo Grounds, then come home to Harlem and hit "four sewers" while playing stickball.) None of us had Willie Mays-like talent, but we did have fans who sat on their stoops or in chairs cheering us and keeping an eye on the traffic. "Watch the cars, watch the cars!" they would yell.

Pigeon racing was also a favorite competitive sport in Ozone Park, and staring up at the ceiling of the Welfare Island hospital, my mind drifted to this as well—perhaps because I longed for the ability to take wing and fly, or at least stand on a rooftop and gaze at an open sky.

Almost every Italian family in our neighborhood had a pigeon coop on the roof where they kept flocks of homing pigeons they had trained to fly away and then find their way back. On Sundays after Mass, the men would drive to a spot a few miles beyond the city limits and open the coops so the birds could soar free, sometimes traveling hundreds of miles. The winner was determined by how many of his own pigeons returned to him, plus how many of his neighbors' birds he could capture. The prize meant bragging rights for the entire week—and boasting about your win was its own competitive sport in Ozone Park.

In today's culture, being recognized as a stickball champion or homing pigeon king might seem silly, but when I was a kid we found fun and enjoyment in much simpler pleasures.

Yet, while we found ways to have fun, I don't want to give you the impression that life was easy for people in Ozone Park in the 1930s. Most of our families, my own included, were hard hit by the Great Depression, which was sparked by the Stock Market crash of 1929, but really took effect in the early 1930s. My father had lost his job, so early each morning he left the house to look for work. There was little to be found. My parents decided that we had to rent out our three bedrooms in order to provide a more reliable income. So all six of us slept on the screened-in porch while tenants slept in the rooms that had been ours. We froze in the winter and sweated in the summer, but we knew that in order to pay the bills, we had to make this sacrifice.

A disturbing memory from the Great Depression has remained with me throughout my life. One morning, a neighbor rushed into our house and told my mother to hurry and withdraw all our money from the bank before it forever shut its doors. How could such a thing happen? Banks didn't close, at least not permanently. We had deposited our meager savings there, assuming the money would be safer in a bank than under a mattress. My mother and I grabbed our coats and ran the ten long blocks to the Richmond Hill Savings Bank on Liberty Avenue. When we arrived, there were hundreds of grim-looking people, many clutching their bank books, milling around the entrance. We waited for what seemed like hours. Finally, the bank manager stepped outside and told us that the bank was closed but might reopen the next day.

Might.

My mother returned the next morning, and the morning after that. Every day for weeks she waited faithfully for the bank to open. It never did. The manager seemed to have disappeared or at least forgotten about us, but people didn't want to take a chance of missing the day when the doors finally opened. I don't remember how many days passed before we realized that the bank would never reopen. Needless to say, we lost whatever small amount of money my parents had managed to save for the "rainy day" that had already arrived.

Another, more joyous memory of this time—and one that helped sustain me during the dark days and nights on Welfare Island—was of a sports event; one that was fraught with significance at the time, and that I doubt many Americans today even remember, much less understand. It was 1938, and although it would be three years before we would actually go to war with them, Nazi Germany and the U.S. were already engaged in a political conflict. The Nazis needed a propaganda victory in the West to showcase their odious racial views. And they felt they had found one in the person of Max Schmeling: The German former world heavyweight champion had defeated American Joe Louis, whose grandparents had been slaves, in twelve rounds in a match in June 1936. Germany hailed Schmeling as a hero and declared his victory as proof that the Aryan race was indeed superior. American fans claimed that Louis hadn't trained seriously for the fight against the German.

A rematch was scheduled at Yankee Stadium for June 22, 1938. This time, Louis prepared for the fight as if his life depended on it. A Nazi party propagandist who accompanied Schmeling to New York declared that a black man didn't have a chance against Schmeling. He also announced that Schmeling would donate his prize money to build tanks for the German war machine.

Schmeling never actually joined the Nazi party and opposed Hitler's claims of racial superiority. "I am a fighter, not a politician. I am no superman in any way," he told reporters. It didn't matter: The world saw Louis-Schmeling as a battle of competing ideologies; sports fans saw it as having all the elements of an epic bout. More than 70,000 onlookers filled Yankee Stadium to watch the fight on a warm, New York night.

In our neighborhood, families set up tables and chairs outside, and we listened anxiously to the broadcast on the radio. While there were many families in Ozone Park whose ancestry could be traced back to Germany, everyone—no matter what their surname—was solidly behind Joe Louis.

This time, the American immediately went on the offensive. In just two minutes and four seconds, he was declared winner by knock-out, and was crowned heavyweight champion of the world. The jubilant uproar in the streets was deafening! We celebrated by banging pots and pans, running through the streets, crying, shouting, yelling Joe Louis' name. I've never experienced such an electric atmosphere. As far as we were concerned in Ozone Park he had fought for all Americans, and for democracy. We knew now that if we had to go to war against Hitler, which was becoming increasingly likely, we would beat the enemy that we had already vanquished here in Yankee Stadium.

I wished, like Joe Louis, I could strike a blow for democracy. But all I could do was lie in the bed on Welfare Island. As I ran through the memories of my life to that point, my thoughts inevitably turned to my family. My misplaced anger for them when I was first diagnosed with TB has long since abated. I realized I loved my parents and sisters, and longed to be back in Ozone Park with them, regardless of our financial circumstances. Don't get me wrong: I wished we had more money. So did my parents. So did nearly everyone in our Depression-ravaged neighborhood. But I realized, once I was away from them, that despite being poor, I had a rich and happy home life. To this day, that realization has made family a priority for me; and also helped me keep the importance of money in perspective. Let's be honest, rich or poor, it's nice to have money. But it's not a substitute for having values in life, and a loving family.

It's funny how insightful one can become when forced to stare at a ceiling for hours on end. Another lesson learned from that time on Welfare Island was just how lucky I was to have parents who in turn had a remarkable ability to get along, no matter what the circumstances. I don't ever remember either them sounding bitter or angry or complaining, not even when my father had to dig ditches to make money (and he literally did dig ditches!). They were always very loving and supportive—a wonderful example of a genuinely happy couple.

We had an extended family, as well, that seemed so far away from Welfare Island, and Grandma McCue was its heart and soul. She was one of a kind, a strong, tough Irish woman who we visited every Sunday. Grandma McCue loved to drink beer and loved to play the horses. She had what she called her "line of credit." She'd string a clothesline above her kitchen sink and pinned all her bills to the line, including her beer tab. The beer bill was, of course, the first to get paid every month. Her bookie was second.

But despite her fondness for the hops and horses, she was also one of the most tenderhearted, tolerant, and patient women I've ever met. I loved going to see her, and my whole extended family—my aunts, uncles, and all my cousins—would always be there, as well.

There was another member of the family always on hand at Grandma McCue's. Father Jolly, a Catholic priest at the local parish, wasn't actually related to us, but he was a fixture at Grandma McCue's Sunday dinner, and thus, as far as we were concerned, was part of our family. He said grace before supper, told us kids spooky stories after we finished eating, and recited the Irish blessing before everyone went home. The kids loved his stories because the scary sounds he made seemed so real. We would gather around Grandma McCue's basement, and then turn off the lights. Father Jolly was a brilliant storyteller, who could create a mental picture as well as Orson Welles: creaking doors; cold, frigid blasts of wind; blood-curdling screams. Father Jolly made them all come alive. He scared the hell out of us. Even at age 18, I remember thinking how I wished he could come to Welfare Island and tell me a story (but of course, as I was quarantined, I couldn't have visitors, which only added to my loneliness).

After every story, Father Jolly taught us a lesson that included a short but important message. I still remember one that has stuck with me all these years later:

"If you died tomorrow, what would you regret not having done while you were alive?"

I still ask myself that question—and one of the answers is why you now have this book in your hands.

After Father Jolly's story, the ritualized evening at Grandma McCue's would end with my Uncle Johnny, who had a beautiful tenor voice, singing "In a Shanty in Old Shanty Town." My mother and my father's sisters would usually cry because the song was so meaningful to them. While I'm glad I never had to live in a shantytown, no amount of money could buy such wonderful memories, and I feel blessed to have experienced them, because they carried me through all my most trying moments.

Especially the ones I was living through as the months of 1942 ticked away. It was bad enough I couldn't fight, I thought—I couldn't even work to support the war effort! And I thought to myself, through gritted teeth, hadn't I already proved that I was a willing and hard worker?

As the only boy of our family, I felt I should help my family as much as possible. I got my first job as a paperboy when I was thirteen. I had to take the bundles of the Long Island Press off the truck, then sort, organize, and deliver them to my customers. I quickly discovered that walking was both tiring and inefficient, so I figured out a better way: I packed the papers in my sister's baby carriage and pushed it all along my route.

I dreamed up another idea, this one in order to sell more papers. I don't know where or how this scheme came to me, but in hindsight I think it was the first inklings of my entrepreneurial instincts. I'd noticed that after my friends and I had grabbed our bundles of freshly printed newspapers off the delivery truck, there was always a pile of papers left over. I began to spend a few minutes every day chatting with the driver, and pretty soon we got to be friendly enough that when I asked him whether it would be okay to take some of the extras, he shrugged and said, "Sure, go ahead, kid."

I grabbed a few papers and neatly folded them. I already knew which families weren't customers, so I'd head for the closest house and ring the bell, all the while pumping up my confidence by telling myself I was about to offer the best present imaginable. As soon as someone appeared, I'd launch into my sales pitch.

"Good afternoon, I'm Walter Scherr, and I want to leave you a paper every day this week. It's totally free, no obligation. I have lots of customers on this street, and they tell me they like getting the grocery inserts (or the sports section or whatever I thought was most likely to appeal to the person at the door). See if you think you're interested. I'll come back next week, and we can talk about whether you want to sign up for delivery."

To my surprise, this worked! I got more and more orders. I learned some great lessons from trudging up and down those streets. Cold calls may seem difficult at first, but they can be very rewarding, as I found out when the Press sponsored a contest to help motivate us to boost our sales (something I was already doing). The prize was a brand-new bicycle, which my parents never could have afforded to buy me. By that point, I was fed up with using a baby carriage. I decided I had to win. I worked overtime cold-calling around the neighborhood. As a result, I was able to meet and beat my sales quota, and sure enough, I won. I now had a brand-new bicycle to make my route more efficient.

By the time of the next contest for Long Island Press, I had perfected my sales strategy, and even developed a more sophisticated strategy. I used current customers—those who had helped me win the first contest—to get referrals. I would then tell these folks that their neighbor found something of interest in the paper, so they might also (I had figured out that people don't like to think that their neighbors know something they might not!). It worked: my prize was a trip to Boston, one of the highlights of my young life. I'd never been out of Ozone Park, much less New York City, so going all the way to Boston, Massachusetts—a city in another state—was a really big deal for me. I went with a couple of my pals, who had also sold more than their quota of newspapers. We stayed at a hotel, another first for me. I don't remember its name, which is just as well, because it probably wasn't much to brag about. But for all we knew, it was the swankiest joint in the city—Boston's version of the Ritz Carlton or the Waldorf Astoria. We were so excited and impressed that we all had to bring something back to show our mothers that our efforts had been suitably rewarded. We'd never seen real silverware before, so each of us, unbeknownst to the other, hid a fork or a spoon or a knife in our pocket to bring home as a souvenir.

After a couple of nights away from home, we thought we were so sophisticated, even though we probably didn't even have one real suitcase among the three of us. More likely, we'd stuck a change of clothes and a toothbrush in a canvas rucksack, maybe something one of our relatives had used during World War I. Whatever we'd done and seen in Boston, we were still the same naive kids who'd arrived two days earlier. We slung our bags over our shoulders and rode down in the elevator. And then, surprise! When the door slid open, a guy the size of Tuffy Leemans stood blocking our way. He pointed to the table next to him. "Hold it boys," he said in a polite but firm voice (one that suggested to me that we weren't the first group of kids to try to abscond with hotel "souvenirs"). "Take everything out of your pockets, please."

It hadn't occurred to us that what we'd done could be construed as stealing. Humiliated and chagrined, each of us reluctantly removed the piece of silverware and carefully placed it on the table. My first thought was whether I'd have to confess on Sunday that I'd committed the sin of stealing. My second thought was whether the man was going to arrest the three of us. But all he said was, "Thank you very much, boys. We hope you enjoyed your stay here."

Whew! I was relieved. The possibility of sinning and having to confess was no laughing matter for me. I was an altar boy at our church, St. Mary Gate of Heaven, on Jerome Avenue and 104th Street in Ozone Park. The downside to being an altar boy in the same church where I made my confession was that all the priests knew me, even behind the curtain of the confession booth. Sometimes I had to leave my place in line and go to the back a few times until I was comfortable with whatever I planned to confess that day. Which, to be honest, wasn't much (luckily, I never had to discuss the Mystery Lady with the parish priest).

All of these memories, from the Joe Louis fight to Grandma McCue, from my parents to my paperboy career, sustained me during the uneventful days in the hospital. But the nights...the nights were torturous. The ward would get so dark that I couldn't see my hand in front of my face. The room reverberated with the sounds of patients choking, drowning in their own fluids, taking their last breath...the death rattle. While we slept—or tried to—orderlies moved from bed to bed, shining flashlights in our faces to check whether we were still alive. They would hurriedly remove the bodies of those who had succumbed, and then they would move on to the next patient and the patient after that. During my first couple of weeks on the ward, I was terrified by the constant noises, the death rattles, the flickering lights. But soon I got used to the ritual, and I would be filled with resentment that yet another death had disturbed my sleep. It was a cold place.

I spent six months on Welfare Island. Then came another move, this time to Otisville, a small town about seventy miles north of New York City. Today, Otisville is home to a New York State medium security prison, but in the mid-1940s, it was known for its public sanatorium, a place for those too poor to afford a private and therefore more luxurious institution.

That's where I was headed in late 1942, as America began to fight back against fascism, on Guadalcanal, at Midway, in North Africa, with guys my age shouldering much of the burden.

Me? I was soon to be 19, but I had nowhere to go but to bed.

THE OTISVILLE ODYSSEY

For tuberculosis patients, Otisville was Devil's Island or Alcatraz. Like those infamous prisons-of-last-resort, only the worst cases ended up here: patients so sick that they were deemed to have only a minimal chance of survival.

The comparison with penitentiaries didn't end there. Otisville looked and smelled like a prison, and it had a list of rules that made me feel more like an inmate than a patient. I wasn't allowed outside because I had TB, and in order to earn any privileges, I had to have negative sputum. All the doctors and nurses were involved in the war effort, so as had been the case on Welfare Island, we had less-than-qualified people to take care of us.

Today, most people know little about TB, as it's been largely eradicated in this country. But even into the early 1940s it was still a scourge; a disease as dreaded as polio. Although scientists had spent years trying to find a cure, an effective antibiotic agent wouldn't be discovered until 1944—two years in the future. In the meantime, I learned that there were only three techniques known to assist the body in healing from TB. The first was complete bed rest. The theory was that staying in bed reduced the pressure on the lungs and allowed them to rest, so that the body would heal itself.

Patients who showed no signs of improvement after prolonged bed rest were subjected to pneumothorax, which involved collapsing the lung. The thinking behind this treatment was that the lung could rest and heal more quickly while it was collapsed and not in use. The procedure was excruciatingly painful: Once a month, a very large needle was inserted into the patient's lung through the patient's side and into the lung in order to collapse it. A fluoroscope, an early version of the x-ray machine, was used to determine whether the lung was healing. In the meantime, the patient had to get along with only one working lung.

If neither bed rest nor pneumothorax was successful, there was the third, least preferable and most traumatic procedure: thoracoplasty, in which the pockets of tuberculosis in the lungs were collapsed by removing the ribs from the chest wall. This was radical surgery, and patients who were subjected to it would be permanently deformed—hunched over on one side because as many as seven or eight ribs would have been cut out in order to remove the affected lung.

During my first year at Otisville, I had my lung collapsed every month. I dreaded seeing the doctor approach my bed, knowing that he was about to stick a needle into my side—a horrible experience. I would grit my teeth and think about how much I hated my life. But eventually I realized that I couldn't get better if I continued to be mired in self-pity. I think my emotional and physical recovery began the day I stopped feeling sorry for myself and started thinking about my two cousins, Anna and Eadie—who lived next door to Grandma McCue—and what they had gone through a few years earlier.

Anna was six and Eadie was seven the day our whole family took a boat ride up the Hudson, a rare treat for us because we so seldom had the money to spend on such frivolous pleasures. We picnicked at Bear Mountain and then headed back to New York. But first, their parents and then the rest of the adults noticed that the two girls seemed unwell, and they were getting worse the closer we got to home. None of the grownups said the word aloud, but we all knew what they were thinking about: the terrifying possibility that the girls had contracted polio. By the time the boat docked in New York, Anna and Eadie had high fevers and couldn't move their muscles. Two ambulances were waiting to rush them to the hospital.

I was old enough to understand how polio could affect their bodies, that they might never be able to breathe on their own and that they could be paralyzed for the rest of their lives. I remember visiting Grandma McCue and going next door, where the two cousins lived, where I saw them lying in the tomb-like iron lungs that enabled them to breathe. All you could see of them was their faces, reflected in the mirrors. Eadie was paralyzed from the neck down, and Anna couldn't walk. If it hadn't been for all the men in our family, who spent hours following the then-famous "Sister Kenny" method for treating polio—applying wet, hot compresses to relieve my cousins' painful muscle spasms and massaging their muscles to prevent them from atrophying—the two girls would have been paralyzed for life.

Anna and Eadie both learned to walk again. They got married, had children, and lived to see their grandchildren. Anna worked at a small company for thirty years and Eadie taught elementary school.

They needed canes for support and wore braces on their legs, but they had tremendous spirit. (Today, Anna is the only one of my cousins who's still alive. When she joined my family for my 90th birthday celebration, I gave her a bracelet that was inscribed "To my hero, from cousin Walter." She replied, "I want to be buried with this bracelet!")

Anna and Eadie were my inspiration and role models. I made up my mind at Otisville that if those two girls could survive their ordeal, which had been far worse and more permanently disabling than mine, I could endure whatever I had to in order to regain my health. It was a resolution that would be tested.

Thanks in part to my new attitude towards fighting the disease, things started to turn around. During my second year at Otisville, I began to feel better and to show negative sputum results. I had survived a whole year there, and had formed friendships with the other patients and the orderlies. Best of all, I still had both lungs and all my ribs intact. My disease had not worsened to the point of last-resort treatment.

I could finally leave the infirmary in a wheelchair and venture for short periods into other parts of the building, including the dining room, where I was allowed to eat three meals a day. This felt like a major triumph.

I was also permitted to have visitors. My devoted mother was the only person who made the long trip north, and she always brought me some small gift—a pair of gloves or a scarf. I was so grateful for her thoughtfulness and generosity. I finally began to believe that my life was taking a turn for the better. I never lost my guilt about not serving in the war, but little by little I was becoming more hopeful about a complete recovery.

By year three, I had gained the privilege of going outside and walking around the grounds without an escort. The world beyond the hospital walls became a place of refuge for me, a break from the institution in which I had spent the last twenty-four months. The fresh air in my lungs and on my skin was such a wonderful sensation that I felt as if I were experiencing it for the first time. I had almost forgotten the glorious colors of nature, and it took a while for my eyes to adjust to the brightness.

Level four came with more rewards and conditions. I was allowed to live in one of the wooden cabins reserved for patients whose health showed signs of improvement. We had a lot more independence living in the cabins than we'd had lying in bed on the wards—and a lot more companionship and fun.

Unfortunately, this almost idyllic period didn't last long. One afternoon I was playing a game of whist with friends when I suddenly started to cough up blood. The bleeding continued for a long time: some days lightly, other days heavily. After it finally stopped, I didn't want to move or even speak for fear of causing another episode. Coughing up blood meant going back to being isolated in bed, losing the taste of freedom I had so recently gained. I was once again a prisoner of tuberculosis. Was this all my life was about? I was ready to give up, because I was tired of fighting to get better, and then having my hopes destroyed. I was terrified that they might have to remove my ribs—the "last-resort" procedure for TB patients—and envisioned myself in a nightmarish future; walking the streets of Ozone Park, hunched over and deformed, as mothers nervously gathered their children close when I staggered by.

By this point, I had been looking forward to going home in a year or so and now...bang! I'm back to square one. I wondered if I really was ever going to beat this thing. Maybe I'd never get out of this hospital. But as I was lying there feeling sorry for myself, I remembered again my cousins Anna and Eadie. Their memory had sustained me during my first weeks at Otisville, and now I latched onto them again. I said to myself, "Those little girls beat polio. They were in a freaking iron lung. If they could do it," I thought, "I can do it."

I also began to chastise myself for having taken such a defeatist view of my situation for so long. Once I'd changed my attitude, I made progress. This latest attack was a setback, granted, but I couldn't let myself slide back into the dark place I'd inhabited for much of the previous two years.

Whether it was the example of my cousins, my new resolve, or just luck, in a week or so the coughing stopped, the bleeding stopped. My throat was clear, and I was back on the road to recovery. Miraculously, through the entire setback my sputum remained negative, which meant that it wasn't so easily transferred to someone else, even though I was coughing up blood. Because of the negative sputum, I was able to resume my place in the cabin on level four.

I was happy that I didn't have to go back to level one. I still had my freedom! The mountainside cabins on the grounds of the sanitarium housed patients who had reached this stage in their recovery. I could walk outside as much as I wanted, but I had to walk up and down the hills every day to strengthen my lungs. It was a test of our overall health if we could make it up and down.

I started to feel a similar sense of companionship, fun, and support from the young men with whom I shared a cabin. I became very close friends with one of them, a fellow named Denny. Our friendship began because we were both sports fanatics. He loved the Yankees as much as I loved the Dodgers, and our happiness depended on whether "our guys" won or lost a game. In addition to our shared enthusiasm for baseball, we were also whist champions, and had a great time competing with the best players in the other cabins.

Denny became the brother I never had, and after our mothers met, they became best friends, too. They really loved each other, and they tried to time their visits so they could spend time together. We liked to tease the two of them about whether they were coming to see us—or each other. What made their friendship, and mine and Denny's, unusual at the time was that he and his mom were African-American (although in those days we used the word "Negroes").

Denny was my first nonwhite friend, and vice versa, but we hardly noticed the difference in our skin color. Later, after we were finally "sprung" from Otisville, I would visit him in Harlem, and he'd come to see me in Ozone Park. Neither of us was ever bothered by any of the people in our neighborhoods, so maybe both communities were more tolerant in those days than they got credit for. As we got older, Denny and I, and our mothers, continued to exchange yearly Christmas cards with news about our families and careers. We eventually lost touch, but I still think about Denny, my Otisville friend and brother.

All of us in the cabins at Otisville had a common goal: to get stronger, healthier, and to stay negative on the daily sputum tests.

Otisville provided an interesting way to measure that: As our health improved, we were assigned to a cabin that was higher up the mountainside, and therefore a longer walk for us to make each day. So our improving health was rewarded with greater exertion: Today, exercise and physical activity is seen as so important to prevention and treatment of many diseases, so I guess despite the fact that they were removing people's ribs and lungs, Otisville was actually ahead of its time in some ways.

With little to occupy our minds, we spent our days and nights planning the best route to climb to the other side of the mountain, where the girls lived. Most of us were in our early twenties, and we knew nothing about sex, except whatever stories we might have heard from older brothers or cousins. We were totally inexperienced and naive, but that didn't stop us from planning our daring exploits. We never actually executed any of our fantasies, because we were afraid we'd get kicked out of the sanatorium. Sure, we were desperate to leave, but only because we were cured, not because we'd been caught acting out some half-baked fantasy.

Long before I was well enough to leave the hospital ward, I'd heard that the administration appointed a "captain" for each cabin, not a boss, but a person whom they trusted to take responsibility for the men who shared his cabin. I knew right away that if—and on my good days, I thought, when—my health improved to the point that I moved into a cabin, I wanted, needed, that job. Maybe my motivation came from being the oldest of four children. I was used to being in charge, and I wanted to remember that feeling in order to reclaim my life in the world. Maybe I was also lured by the prospect of getting paid—not much, ten dollars a month, if I recall correctly. But that money meant I could leave Otisville with something in my pocket. I wouldn't have to arrive home penniless and totally dependent on my parents.

My dream became a reality when I was declared a "level five" patient. My duties as captain included reminding my cabinmates that we had to keep the cabin clean and tidy. I also had to take their temperatures every day, give them their nightly dose of cod liver oil, and keep a record of how everyone was feeling. And I had to fulfill these responsibilities with enough good humor and ease that the other men didn't resent me for being too bossy or controlling. In fact, I even took care to get special tomato juice for the ones who whined about having to take the foul-tasting fish oil.

I didn't realize it at the time, but just as my experience cold-calling for the Long Island Press had taught me some valuable lessons in salesmanship, the managerial skills and confidence I gained as a captain in the Otisville cabins provided the foundation for later on in life. One of the most important was the value of having a clearly-articulated, common goal; one that everyone—employees and management—can strive towards together. For my "team" at Otisville, getting healthy and going home was the mission, and all of us worked together to help accomplish that. In retrospect, and thanks largely to those last few years, my time in Otisville was less like a prison, and more like a sort of military Boot Camp; a crucible of learning, experience, and brotherhood. My fellow patients and I bonded with one another, creating our own small community. We had to adhere to a strict set of rules, but if we followed them and showed improvement we were given greater latitude and responsibility. It wouldn't be long before I was released, and as welcome as that day would be, it was fraught with its own worries and concerns. Would I have the social skills to reconnect with the world beyond Otisville, when all I'd known for years was how to live here? How would I get a job to support myself? Who would want to hire me, an ex-TB patient, when so many men returning from the war needed to find work? What about my old friends from Ozone Park, all the guys who'd fought overseas? Would they welcome me back? And would I ever meet a woman who could accept and love me with all my limitations?

In that sense, I guess my Otisville attitude remained very much like that of a prisoner. Like prisoners who had become accustomed to their lack of freedom, we wondered whether we would be better off staying in jail, because we were frightened by the idea of functioning on the outside.

HOME AGAIN

My discharge day finally arrived in the summer of 1948—nearly seven years after I'd first been diagnosed with TB at the Whitehall recruiting station. I was handed twenty dollars to take the bus back to New York. I wanted to surprise my parents, so I didn't tell them I was coming home. I got back to Queens around supper time, and I was so excited to see everyone that I burst through the back door into the kitchen. I got the surprise of my life: total strangers were sitting at the table in my kitchen! It turned out that my parents had moved around the corner, and my mother hadn't told me because she wanted to surprise me! Fortunately, the people who had bought our house knew all about me, so they told me where my family was now living. I hurried over to our new home, not quite as enthusiastic about the surprise element, but still very excited. I was finally back home!

I had waited years for this day, hardly daring to believe it would actually happen. I had returned to a world that felt totally unfamiliar to me. World War II had ended, as had my own private war with tuberculosis. The soldiers coming back from the war were expected to reclaim their old lives as if time had stood still and nothing had changed since Pearl Harbor, neither on the home front nor on the battlefield. I, too, had to reestablish my identity as the kid from Ozone Park who was always ready for fun, adventure, and finding a way to earn some bucks. But unlike the soldiers, I had no medals or scars or tales of terror or courage under fire to show for the war I had fought.

Which one of those guys—genuine heroes in the fight against fascism—would want to associate with me? Why would a veteran of D-Day or Iwo Jima hang around with a guy who'd fought the Battle of Otisville? I imagined a life of loneliness, of no friends outside of my family.

It turned out that my childhood friends, recently back from Europe and the Far East, welcomed me without reservations. My history of TB didn't faze them after they'd risked their lives in combat! On the other hand, people who met me for the first time and were ignorant about TB treated me like a leper. Some of my neighbors would even cross the street when they saw me rather than say hello. It was painful, but I also understood their reasoning. Tuberculosis was a communicable disease without an easy cure, and they didn't want to risk catching it from me. For that reason, I was required to report to the Board of Health every month. I had to take a 40-minute bus ride to Jamaica, during which my imagination would run wild. I'd worry, worry, worry that the fatigue I'd felt, the pound of weight I'd lost since the last time I'd stepped on a scale, were all harbingers of a return of the dreaded disease. By the time I would arrive in Jamaica, my seat on the bus would be covered in sweat. My fears were unfounded: The x-rays and sputum tests kept coming back negative, and the frequency of my mandatory visits decreased.

Finally, the letters TB were no longer associated with my life. Instead, I had a new, three-letter challenge. Finding a J-O-B. In those years, most places expected to be interviewing veterans. A job candidate who had not served, for whatever reason, was usually met with a raised eyebrow and a frosty "sorry, we have no openings."

Just because some people (and employers) didn't want to see me, that didn't mean I couldn't still enjoy my neighborhood. During my tedious and frustrated job hunt, I visited my old haunts regularly, including a luncheonette I knew on Liberty Avenue and 108th Street that was owned by two brothers, Henry and Fritz. I'd been going there since I was a kid. One day, not long after returning from the sanitarium, I went in for a "two cents plain"—a delicious, inexpensive, and now sadly forgotten concoction of seltzer with chocolate syrup. It was the smoothie of its day, except nobody made any pretense of its nutritional value. Who cared? It was delicious—and affordable.

This was the first time Henry and Fritz had seen me since Pearl Harbor, and they asked me where I'd been, no doubt expecting to hear a response like, "France," "the Solomons," or even "Japan." They didn't blink when I told them the truth. "Glad you're back, kid," said Fritz, as he handed me my two cents plain. As I sat there sipping it, I watched people coming in and out. The place was busy, way busier than I'd remembered it. This was true all over in the late 1940s. The Depression was clearly behind us, and the post-war economy was humming. I watched Henry and Fritz flying around the store, trying to cook, serve, work the cash register, and chat with their customers. "Gee, Henry," I said, when he finally had a second to stand still. "You could use some help here." Henry looked at me. "We sure could, Walter," he replied. And then he paused a second as if sizing me up.

"You interested?"

Voila! I had my first job.

In my mind's eye, I can still see Henry and Fritz's luncheonette. Similar establishments—also called "ice cream parlors," although they served a lot more than ice cream—dotted the avenues of New York City in those days. They had a candy counter and a soda fountain with high stools. In the back, there were tables and a booth. The floor was checkerboard, there were mirrors behind the soda fountain, and the big brass cash register on the counter was crowded with little knickknacks for sale. On summer days, the lazily-rotating blades of a big fan on the ceiling kept the customers (relatively) cool in the pre-air-conditioning era. It was always fanatically clean.

I worked from 7 a.m. to 2 p.m., six days a week. I scrambled eggs and poured coffee for the truck drivers and deliverymen who came in for breakfast, I cleaned tables at lunch, I learned to make ice cream floats, and I could whip up a mean two cents plain. I also saw how

Henry and Fritz treated their customers and me as the employee. In a word: well. I saw the effect it had, too. Their customers were loyal, and so was I.

One day, Fritz made a shocking announcement. He was leaving the business, and going into a monastery. Almost unheard of today, it was rare even in a heavily Catholic neighborhood in the 1940s. As an altar boy, I certainly wouldn't question anyone's urge to serve the Lord, but I must admit I was curious why Fritz would leave our wonderful, close-knit community, his successful business, and his loved ones. But that was a tough, even impertinent question for me to ask, so I kept my mouth shut.

The day Fritz left, we had a party. The truck drivers were there. The lunchtime customers popped up. Everyone in the neighborhood, anyone who'd enjoyed a two cents plain, a burger, or just some pleasant small talk with Fritz showed up. Near the end of the party, he took me aside. A short, stocky guy who looked like he could have been a fullback, he put his arm around me. He knew that I didn't really understand why he was leaving. "Walter," he said. "there's more to life than just building a business. Nobody lives forever. You have to make an accounting of your life." He had decided that the way he was going to do this was to enter the monastery and pray for other people. Fritz's dedication to a higher purpose had an effect on me. As I would begin to climb the business ladder, I continually tried to keep in mind the fact that there was more to life than the rungs of that ladder.

The truck drivers who showed up for Fritz's farewell party had also become friendly with me. Back then, there was a whole category of truckers you don't really see today: milkmen, bread deliverymen, coal delivery guys who distributed their wares not to the local 7-11 (there were none in those days), but directly to the home.

I remember that these guys, most of them veterans, seemed to have a lot of pride in what they were doing. The driver for Dugan's—a big commercial bakery in the New York area—would always tell us how good his products were. He used to be so excited when he'd pick up another customer—basically, another housewife in Ozone Park or Richmond Hill. He was proud of the special service he'd give them. Whether you put the bread on the right side or the left side of the door made a difference in sales. Right was more visible, and so he did. But I think simply the fact that he'd somehow learned or researched this fact—about something as arcane as the way in which people would pick up bread left on their doorstep!—impressed me.

Looking back, I realize that as opposed to being merely employees, these deliverymen were entrepreneurs. So was Henry, who never took a class in consumer behavior, but could have taught one. As you'd go up to the cash register at his place, fishing into your wallet or purse, Henry made sure to have something eye-catching but inexpensive near the register. It could be gum, or some brightly wrapped candies. Often, it was cookies, made by Henry's wife—even she had a role in the business. I would observe the customers as they'd leave. On the spur of the moment, most of them would buy one of these items on impulse. Henry wouldn't push too hard, either. But sometimes he'd give the customer a gentle nudge. He'd notice a customer eyeing the cookies. "Try one," he say. "My wife baked 'em this morning."

"Why not?" was the usual response. Ka-ching, went the big brass cash register. Another sale for Henry and Fritz.

They saw opportunities to make money, while giving customers quality service and products. I learned a lot about business in that humble little luncheonette. But the most important one, perhaps, was the gift of generosity and giving back.

Henry and Fritz felt that I was college material. They knew I wanted to continue my education, too, but couldn't afford it. They told me one afternoon that they had discussed this and come up with a new policy. From now on, all the tips in the store were going to be put in a jar for Walter's college fund. Even on days I didn't work, they and the rest of the staff dutifully contributed their nickels and dimes. I'd like to say it was because of my winning personality, but I think the real reason was that they knew my story, and wanted to help out a kid from the neighborhood who'd endured some hard times.

Eventually, we collected enough money for me to register for night classes at Pace Institute. I don't think anything would have made them happier to see that, thanks to the education at their luncheonette and at Pace (both of which they essentially paid for), I would end up being a founding board member of five multi-national companies. I worked for Henry and Fritz's for four years. That's not very long in the scheme of a nine-decade life, but those four years were as valuable as the years I'd spent in college. You never know where you'll learn lessons that will last a lifetime. And to think it all started with a two cents plain.

Armed with my certificate in accounting from Pace it was time now to move on from being a 28-year-old soda jerk. I didn't know where to start looking for a real job; just the word career scared me. My mother and a former tenant of ours deserve the credit for kick-starting my career. My mother suggested that I locate our tenant, who very obligingly wrote me the referral letter I needed to get started. I randomly chose an employment agency, which sent me for an interview at the Sperry Gyroscope Company. The person in personnel at Sperry needed someone to fill the job of junior accountant. I showed up with my letter of reference and my Pace certificate, so he hired me. I think the fact that I was breathing and could add two plus two was sufficient criteria as far as they were concerned at the time. They had a thousand people in Sperry's accounting department, and all of them were busy keeping up with the demand of their fast-growing business. Everything was done by hand since there was no technology yet to do those jobs.

Things seemed to be falling in place for me, at long last. I now had a job (albeit a lowly one) in a major corporation. I had a certificate from a two-year higher education institution. I still had my friends. Just one more part of the puzzle remained for the former sanitarium patient, and in many ways it was the most nerve-wracking. A lot of my Ozone Park buddies were now married. But here I was in my late twenties and had never even had a girlfriend. What would I have to offer a woman, anyway? I didn't have any money, a car, or even a good story to tell of where I'd been during the war.

One afternoon, I came home and found my sister Janet sitting in our kitchen eating corn on the cob with a friend of hers, Vera Kessler. They'd known each other since elementary school, and I'd never paid much attention to her while I was growing up. But suddenly, I saw her with new eyes—the girl from the neighborhood had grown up to be a beautiful, smart, accomplished woman. She even had a big-time job, working as the private secretary to General Lucius Clay, who had overseen the 1948-49 Berlin Airlift, when the Soviets had attempted to blockade West Berlin.

Even gnawing away at a piece of corn on the cob, she looked beautiful to me, and my shocked look must have given me away, as both she and Janet looked at each other and giggled. To be honest, I'm still not sure exactly how or why it happened—at that point in our lives, how could a woman like her possibly have been interested in a guy like me?—but soon we were dating, and a few years later, in 1953, we would be married. I had no money to pay for the wedding, so Vera did. She paid for everything because she believed in me wholeheartedly.

Actually, I did make a contribution to the wedding reception: I paid for the champagne. Or at least I passed it off as champagne. Because I couldn't afford the real bubbly, I added Alka Selzer to some inexpensive wine and passed it off to everyone at the reception as champagne. The amazing thing, in retrospect, is that no one seemed to notice or care. Or maybe they were too busy whispering behind our backs.

"How could that beauty, Vera Kessler, working for General Lucius Clay, marry a soda jerk?" I'm sure that's what some people were thinking as they sipped their faux champagne. And since none of my Ozone Park buddies would say it to my face at the time, I used to say it for them. In fact, I think it's still true today:

I married above my pay grade.

A LOT TO LEARN AT SPERRY

SPERRY GYROSCOPE HAD BEEN FOUNDED IN 1910 BY ELMER SPERRY, one of the most brilliant and prolific inventors of the early 20th century. Sperry himself held nearly 400 patents—about twice as many as Thomas Edison—including the gyro-compass, which dramatically improved the navigation and stability of ships. His company, housed in a Brooklyn factory, manufactured gyroscope-related products. By the time I was hired as a junior accountant, Sperry was a huge corporation, located in the town of Lake Success, and was one of three major defense contractors based on Long Island.

During World War II, Sperry employed between 22,000 and 30,000 people to produce a wide range of war-related equipment, including the Boeing B-17 Flying Fortress (equipped with its famous ball turret gun), and what were then considered such technological advances as airborne radar and automated landing systems. I was so grateful to be hired by such a colossus that I didn't mind being a junior accountant in a 1,000-person department. My "desk" was a piece of plank that rested on saw horses, and I spent my days posting ball-bearing account inventory on a 1940s predecessor to the calculator called a comptometer, a key-driven, manual machine that performed basic arithmetic functions. The work was easy, if sometimes monotonous, and my salary was $75 a week. Sperry treated its employees well and offered great benefits, including a very generous full reimbursement of tuition expenses. Excited by the prospect of a free education, I enrolled in night classes and earned my B.A. from Pace College. (I eventually received a Master's degree from Hofstra University, and became a doctoral student at New York University, all at Sperry's expense, for which I am still grateful.)

After six years in Otisville and then working as a soda jerk, I was eager to move ahead as quickly as possible. I was encouraged to learn that Sperry preferred to promote from within, and that they made a point of identifying employees who they felt could be "fast-tracked" into managerial positions.

Having lost all those years in the sanitarium, I wanted to be on the fastest track possible. As it turned out, something I'd read while passing the hours in the Otisville cabins five years earlier gave me the knowledge to hit the ground running at Sperry. It was a book that explained, of all things, the unequal distribution of wealth in Italy. The author was an economist named Vilfredo Pareto, who had observed in the early 1900s that 80 percent of the land in his native country was owned by 20 percent of the population. Also known as the "law of the vital few," Pareto's 80/20 Principle eventually became a cornerstone of many businesses, and is taught today in MBA programs around the country.

While the 80/20 Principle is now applied in many areas of business, Pareto's book was just beginning to catch on in the post-war years. As someone who had read his book—and I had done so only out of boredom at Otisville!—I recognized that it could be applied to my new job at Sperry in the inventory group. It was one of those "a-ha" moments we all have in life. Somehow I gathered up enough courage to ask for a lunch meeting with the manager of the department to share my thoughts about how to make our operation more efficient, using the insight found not on the production line or through management experience, but while lying in a bed in a sanitarium. Some bosses would have dismissed me out of hand: "Who do you think you are? You have no working experience outside of a luncheonette, and you're going to tell us, one of the largest defense contractors in America, how we can improve our business?" Instead, when I nervously explained Pareto and the idea of the 80/20 rule to him over lunch and how I thought it could apply to us, he nodded thoughtfully. "Interesting," he said. "I like it!" He assigned me to work with a 30-year Sperry veteran named Jimmy Drew to help implement my idea.

Essentially, my thinking was that by concentrating on the 20 percent of the parts that were responsible for 80 percent of the costs in our department, we could reduce the head count of our department by 20 percent. These employees could then be reassigned to other areas of Sperry. Working with Drew—who, despite his vastly senior status, embraced the idea and treated me like an equal—we instituted a control program to track every step of the process of the vital parts, again following Pareto's dictate of the "vital few and trivial many," and tracked the defective parts that could help us make the manufacturing process more efficient.

It worked. For the first time in my life, I felt like my star was rising. Moreover, the seemingly lost and lonely hours at Otisville had actually yielded something useful to me. Also, I realized that I was finally in the right place at the right moment. As a direct result of the Cold War that was already developing in the aftermath of our defeat of the Nazis and Japanese, the Defense Department was now taking a greater interest in Sperry than they had at any time since 1945. They were concerned about the possibility of enemy—now meaning Russian—attacks. They didn't want all of Sperry's defense equipment production to be concentrated in one place, so they asked us to diversify our facilities by opening ten factories throughout the United States.

In the course of two years, I was on the fast track and appointed Director of Cost Accounting. They wanted me to have experience in other departments as well, so I was soon appointed Director of Planning, Procedures, and Organization.

Here, I was managing thirty people, ten of whom worked on parking procedures alone. Keep in mind that at this time, the vast majority of Sperry's 30,000 employees commuted by car to the company's Lake Success plant. That's a lot of parking spaces! Not surprisingly it led to a lot of parking-related issues. Who got to park where? In which lots? With what stickers and clearance? It was a big and ongoing job.

Still, I couldn't help thinking that even given the importance of employee parking, the idea of having one-third of the employees in my department working on parking didn't make sense. We're supposed to be defending the Free World. But we have thirty people focused on parking?

Time again for the 80/20 principle to be applied! I decided that as the top 600 executives of Sperry represented 20 percent of the total number of managers, I would simply allocate to those people parking spaces according to the criteria that were established, i.e., salary, responsibility, disability, tenure. Yes, some people would have to change parking spaces, maybe even move a couple of rows further away, but weighed against the benefits to the company, I doubted anybody would be mightily inconvenienced. The idea was to make the business operate more efficiently, right? Besides, this would also reduce the ten people in my department working on parking to only four, allowing the remaining six to work on other company projects. This made so much sense, I thought, as I sat back contentedly in my chair. Way to go, Walter! How did Sperry ever get along without me? I congratulated myself and then released the new procedure throughout the organization.

The very next day, I got a call from Blanche, the secretary for the president. He wanted to see me immediately. I practically bounced on the elevator up to the fourth floor executive suites. I was sure that I was being summoned by the president in grateful recognition of how, in one simple stroke, I had solved a problem that had bedeviled the organization for years. Surely he wanted to know, who was this young and upcoming talent, Walter J. Scherr? Perhaps he'd even promote me on the spot!

I was ushered by Blanche into the inner sanctum of the man who ran one of the largest defense contractors in the United States. He had a reputation for being a bit cranky even in the best of times, so I didn't expect him to be overly effusive in his praise, as he handed me my bonus check and my promotion. Luckily, Walter J. Scherr came from modest beginnings. He didn't need applause as he climbed the ladder of success.

What I didn't expect was that the president was armed with a saw, ready to cut off the rungs.

He looked up when I entered the office.

"You're Scherr?" he asked gruffly.

"Yes, sir," I replied, standing straight at attention, just in case he wanted to pin a medal for management ingenuity on my chest.

"You're the man who came up with the new parking scheme?" he said, holding up a folder that I immediately recognized as my handi-work. It seemed dog-eared as if he had spent hours savoring the simple brilliance of its words.

"I'm the man!" I said proudly.

His eyes narrowed.

"You, Scherr, are a complete idiot!"

I gulped. "W...what?"

"In fact, you might be the dumbest son of a bitch I have ever had working for me. Do you realize what you have done with this cock-eyed idea?"

"I...I thought I was making things more efficient for us, sir."

"Efficient?" he said, and I could see the veins pulsing in his head. "EFFICIENT?"

"Yes, sir," I continued, unwisely. "I read this in a book on man-agement theory..."

The fingers in his left hand closed into a fist, as the words ex-ploded through clenched teeth. "You read....in a book...on..." the last words were a hiss. "Management...THEORY?"

"Yes, sir."

"Well STOP reading and START listening to me...now."

He picked up a large...very large...stack of small sheets of paper. I recognized them as the missed-call sheets we would get, in the days before voice mail. "These are all from this morning, Scherr. These are people, angry people and, I might add, important people at this company who suddenly learned today that they can't get their parking space at the company they have worked at for decades. They're all screaming at me. And do you know what they want?"

I hung my head in shame, as I tried to formulate the correct response. I noticed the beautifully upholstered rug of the presidential suite. I had imagined my new office would have a rug like this.

"They...they...want their parking spots back?"

"Of course they want their spots back, you fool! But what they want even more, what they're demanding from me, is..."

I looked up.

"Your...head...on...a...PLATE."

Again, my eyes shot down in shame. The president stood up and stabbed a finger in the air...directed at my head, I thought.

"And I have every mind to give it to them!"

At that moment, I wondered if Fritz and Henry had kept my old spot opened at the ice cream parlor. It wouldn't be so bad, I began to rationalize...

"But I'm not going to."

I looked up again, blinking. "Excuse me, sir?"

"I'm not going to fire you, Scherr. But I'll tell you what you're going to do. You're going to go back to your office and you're going to rescind this imbecilic order of yours, and then you're going to call these people back...every single one of them...personally, and apologize and tell them what a stupid idea it was, and that you don't know what you were thinking and that effective immediately they can have their old spots back!"

He handed me the stack of messages. There must have been a hundred slips of paper.

"Oh and Scherr..." he said, as I spun around to leave.

"Yes sir?"

"You know that lot out by the maintenance garage?"

I did—it was the Siberia of parking at Sperry, convenient to our building and grounds people, but what seemed like a mile away from any of the main buildings.

"That's where you're parking from now on."

****

It's odd, isn't it, how things in life shift and turn? Chastened but wiser from the parking debacle—I had learned the importance of building consensus with new ideas, no matter how much sense the idea made, before unilaterally acting alone—I forged ahead in my new job, and managed to stay out of the president's office for awhile. Yet, I must have favorably impressed someone, because not long after that, I was entrusted with something more vital than employee parking.

The Defense Department decreed that Sperry should decentralize in the event of a national emergency. My first decision was to hire a top-flight management consulting firm with vast experience in management relocation. The assignment was huge—decentralize the entire operation and relocate plant sites throughout the country.

This time, I didn't make any impetuous actions.

"Tell me what I don't know," was the first thing I said to them. "Because there's a lot I don't know."

They were initially taken aback by my candor; I sensed that they were used to clients who started off by telling them how much they already knew!

But I had learned—from the bitter experiences of my earlier life, not to mention the parking fiasco—that I didn't have all the answers. Far from it. In this case, I couldn't possibly have accomplished such a complicated task without advice from the consultants I'd hired.

We decentralized the divisions according to areas of technology. One of the most crucial issues was where to locate these newly formed divisions. We needed a steady supply of technically-minded people, so we had to be near university towns. We also needed to be close to an airport, to ensure easy travel from our headquarters on Long Island.

Gainesville and Clearwater, Florida; Salt Lake City, Utah; Huntsville, Alabama; and Phoenix, Arizona, were among the places where Long Island Sperry employees would now be sent. While these are all among the most desirable Sunbelt locations today, that perception did not exist in the 1950s. Getting lifelong New Yorkers to transition to these new communities in what they perceived as being remote parts of the South and far West was very difficult; even traumatic. It wasn't the culture in those days. Many of them had grown up in Queens, Brooklyn, or the

Bronx. Now we were asking them to start anew, but this time in locations thousands of miles away. It was as if we were asking them to move halfway around the world. They were angry about having to turn their lives upside down; heartbroken and anxious about having to find new homes, schools, friends, and churches.

I certainly could relate to this, coming from my close-knit neighborhood in Ozone Park, where friends and families were never more than a bus stop or two away. I remembered what a big deal it was when Fritz, the co-owner of the luncheonette where I worked, had left for the monastery in the South. He might as well have been moving to the Moon as far as people in Ozone Park were concerned! At least he was leaving of his own accord. Here, our employees were being wrenched from places they'd known their entire lives and sent to parts unknown. Unfortunately I was the messenger who spread the life-changing news, disrupting so many of our employees' lives.

I understood why it had to be done and did my best to explain to these employees why the move was necessary, and to make the transition as easy as possible.

While it was a tremendous opportunity to learn about Sperry's diverse products, my life was also disrupted. I was away from home a lot, which was hard on Vera and our growing young family. We would eventually have four children: Douglas, Walter, Jr. (known then and now as Bud), Laura, and Robert. I missed them all terribly while I was on my travels. When I was close enough to home, I'd fly back to New York for the weekend. But those were few and far between. On those weekends when I did make it back to Long Island, I'd return to whichever city I was then based in with huge boxes of bagels and cannolis. These were real treats, tastes of home that unlike today couldn't be found outside of New York, and when I brought them into the factory, they'd disappear before I could even get a cup of coffee.

In addition to the decentralization of its facilities, the Polaris Program, the Navy's nuclear-armed ballistic missile system, was another key factor in my success at Sperry. In 1955, when the Navy announced the creation of the Polaris program, I knew we would submit a bid to produce its navigational systems. But I was eager to do much more. I set up a meeting with Sperry's president. This was a different man than the one that had reamed me out about parking—he was younger, an innovator, and, I knew, more willing to listen. Yet, even though I knew him and his attributes, what I was asking for was big and it was my initiative. In other words, the corporate version of a cold call. I felt for a moment like the 13-year-old boy selling subscriptions to the Long Island Press.

This time when I walked into the president's office, I was confident. But unlike the last time, it was a confidence rooted in having listened and learned before I came up with a plan.

First I talked about my idea. "I want to see Sperry not only producing the navigational equipment, but also managing the whole navigational system," I told him. "All the subcontractors will report to us, and we will report directly to the Navy." I paused a second. "And I'd like you to consider me for the position of director for the entire project."

"Do you think we can do it?" asked the president.

"I'll do whatever's necessary to make it work," I assured him.

The risk was huge, but if we could run a successful program—

and I was convinced we could—Sperry would add another important dimension to its capabilities in the United States' defense effort. It was a daring undertaking, unlike anything we'd done before. He said yes.

A decade after Pearl Harbor, and in a very different kind of conflict, I finally had an opportunity to serve my country.

We built a new plant in Syosset, Long Island, to house the Polaris program. Graduates of Annapolis and West Point were hired as part of our team, and proved to be valuable assets. We poured our hearts and souls into the program. Early on, we struggled to produce enough of the spare parts needed to maintain the submarines. We were very aware that Navy submarine personnel had to be supplied with whatever they needed while they were submerged in far-away locations under dangerous circumstances.

It was also my first interaction with someone famous. Admiral Hyman Rickover was one of two top-ranking naval officers to whom I had to report, and who is considered today to be the father of the modern nuclear submarine program. Perhaps he would have treated me differently if we had been discussing strategy or naval tactics or technologies. But my agenda when I met with the Admiral was always the same: to explain why we needed more money.

Rickover, one of the first to understand how the Navy could use nuclear power, is an important figure in modern military history. Although he was admired for his intelligence, high standards, and integrity, the Admiral had a reputation for being difficult, especially with defense contractors. He would leave me for long hours sitting on a bench outside his office waiting to see him. When he finally found time to see me, he interrogated me as if I were a POW or a warrant officer who'd gone AWOL with a suitcase full of naval secrets.

"Why do you need more money? What kind of crooks are you Sperry guys? Are you meeting the production goals you promised us? How much more is this going to cost the Navy?" The fact was that we were pushing the state of the art to its limits and developing technologies that had never been developed before with many unknowns.

Admiral William Raborn, Jr. was the naval officer in charge of developing a submarine-launched ballistic missile. He had a very different management style. He understood every aspect of the project, and he believed in recognizing the accomplishments of people who worked for him, even if we were contractors!

Admiral Raborn created a team spirit among the defense contractors. If we were behind on a job, he would remind us that by such-and-such a date, "we were supposed to have built ten units, but we've only finished seven." The fact that he included himself—"we"—instead of pointing an accusing finger at us—"you"—made a huge difference to all of us. Admiral Raborn never accused us of failing to do our job, but he reminded us that the Polaris program was critical to the defense of the free world, and that it was up to us to ensure it succeeded. When we told him some equipment parts had been delayed in arriving, he'd say, "We have people under the Arctic Ocean, and they'll be in big trouble if you can't get hold of the spares."

It was hard to say no or come up with mundane excuses when our men were out there submerged in Arctic waters! Knowing that we were dealing with life and death consequences inspired us to be more focused and work harder than ever before. The Navy had ordered the Polaris system to be fully operational by 1965, but under Admiral Raborn's direction, it was ready three years ahead of schedule.

As controller, I understood that out of necessity we sometimes had to begin a job—and therefore spend money for parts and labor—in advance of receiving a signed contract. This was considered risky, because if the contract did not come through it was a company loss. We accommodated the military's requests that defense-related items be available at the earliest possible date. I zealously tracked all of our expenditures, and sent a memo to the production managers prior to reaching our funding limit.

My division president and the vice president of sales could never understand why I was so strict about following company procedures. As soon as I sent out one of my "thirty day" memos, they'd come barging into my office. The question was always the same: "Can't you let it go for once?" My answer was always the same: I couldn't. It was my obligation as caretaker and officer of the company to secure the company's assets.

One time, however, they convinced me to make an exception when we had agreed to undertake a very big project for the Navy. We had no doubt that the project would be ours when the funding was approved; it had been "sole sourced," meaning Sperry was the only company with the technology to produce that particular item. But without a signed contract, we needed permission from Sperry's president before we could spend even a dime on the project. He okayed a $300,000 advance, which at that time was a huge amount of money. Our people in Washington were confident that the contract was a done deal, but I felt uneasy about taking such a big risk. I budgeted the $300,000 to last through a three-month period.

At the end of the three months, the contract hadn't arrived, so I glanced at my figures one more time. Then I walked over to the president's office and told him I'd have to issue an alert that we would stop production. As I'd expected, he summoned the marketing VP and gave him the bad news.

"Walter, I just came back from Washington," the vice president said. "I saw the contract sitting on the guy's desk. He's about to sign it! Why are you so worried? Why can't you ever be a team player?"

I wanted to be liked. I wanted to be a team player. So I gave in. I told myself that this one time, I wouldn't send out the notice. Just this one time. Then I watched as we continued to spend money and wait for a signed contract that never arrived. Within two months we had overrun our budget by hundreds of thousands of dollars.

One of my responsibilities as a financial officer of the company was to present a quarterly status of every in-house project in our division. I had charts that showed project status of approved expenditures, the actual numbers, and reasons for any deviation as to why the project hadn't met the objectives, as well as any corrective action to ensure the objectives would be met. I prided myself on always being very well prepared. But I had no idea how I would respond if anyone asked me about Authorization #72035 (yes, I still remember that number). We were two quarters into it, we'd spent six hundred thousand dollars, but we still didn't have a signed contract.

The only strategy I'd come up with for the board meeting was to talk fast and turn the page, then quickly move on to the next project. But I must not have talked fast enough. One of the Board members waved his hand at me and said, "Walter, go back to the previous page. What's happening with that project?"

I stammered through what I knew was a very weak excuse for why we hadn't adhered to policy. Meanwhile, the two guys who had urged me to authorize the expenditures never said a word. I glanced in their direction, hoping they'd read my mind: Come on, guys! Jump in any time. They kept their mouths shut, their faces blank.

"Weren't you there?" somebody asked them.

The group president shrugged. "We were sure the contract would come in, and Walter didn't emphasize the importance of sending out the notice," he said.

An out and out lie! I looked at him, mouth agape. The Board members didn't know the truth—and didn't bother to try and find out. They had heard enough. The Chairman of the Board lashed out at me. "Walter, do you think you're the smartest accountant in the company? You're not. We gave you this job because we trusted you to watch out for Sperry's corporate interests, not because we needed a team player. You exceeded your authority, and I'm going to call a full Board meeting next week to discuss how you totally mishandled this situation."

I had only myself to blame for letting those two guys totally con me and then throw me under the bus. It was my responsibility—my obligation as the caretaker—to protect Sperry's financial interests. I had known then, as surely as I know now, that I should have been ready to shut down the project. I had ignored everything I'd ever learned about being a trustworthy employee, a successful manager, and perhaps most important, a person who could distinguish between right and wrong.

I went home and lived through what was probably the worst weekend of my career. I couldn't eat or sleep. I had only one thing on my mind. I was about to lose my job, and I would never find another one. My worst nightmare—that I wouldn't be able to take care of my wife and children—was about to come true. I'd watched my parents' struggles during the Depression, and I still felt the shaming sting of being known as a "Relief kid." But nothing my parents had done had caused us to be poor. I, on the other hand, had failed my family by ignoring my conscience. How could I ever forgive myself for such a serious lapse in judgment?

Looking back on that weekend, I'm amazed that Vera didn't pack up the kids and visit her parents for a couple of days just to get away from my moaning and groaning. By Monday morning, I was a total wreck. As I got ready for work on Monday morning, my wife reminded me for the umpteenth time that I'd overcome much worse circumstances, starting with the TB diagnosis. No matter what happened, even if I got fired, Vera said, she loved and believed in me, and she knew that we could handle the consequences of whatever the Board decided about me.

Driving the same route I'd taken so often all the years I'd worked at Sperry, I told myself to keep the faith. Even though I felt like a failure, I had to stop tormenting myself and focus instead on the many blessings in my life, beginning with my wife and children.

I exited the highway, turned onto the road that led to Sperry's plant, and realized that something—an accident or some emergency repairs—was preventing traffic from moving any further. Starting about a block away from the plant, barriers had been set up all along Union Turnpike. Police officers stood on both sides of the highway, so that not only cars, but also pedestrians, couldn't get any closer. After I showed one of the cops my Sperry identification card, he told me that the union, which represented the plant workers, had gone out on strike because their request for a wage increase of eighteen cents an hour had been denied. But instead of encouraging an orderly demonstration, the strikers were overturning cars on the highway, smashing their windows, cutting the tires. People had been injured, some of them badly enough to be rushed to area hospitals.

The situation was so dangerous that even the top executives were being turned away from Sperry's sprawling million-and-a-half square foot building. "Might as well go home," the cop said. "You got yourself a day off."

I disagreed with the union's violent tactics, but I understood their anger. The man who was then president of Sperry's entire operation—the same man who had reamed me in the meeting—kept himself very much apart from the workers. He confided only in his peer group, a handful of people. It never would have occurred to him to visit the plant or even pretend to take an interest in the employees who worked on the ground floor factory.

"Us against them," was the motto of both sides, which meant the strike was going to be a long and bitter one. About a week after it began, two hundred management employees, surrounded by a police escort, were allowed inside. We showed up every day for the next four months, but we didn't have much to do, because nothing was being produced.

After a few weeks I stopped worrying about getting fired. The company's main concern was the strike, and whether the negotiations were moving forward. Nobody, least of all the President of the Board of Directors, had time to think about overspending or an unsigned contract.

About three months into the strike, someone I knew from the contracts department walked into my office and dropped some papers onto my desk. "You'll want to read this," he said.

The signed contract for Authorization #72035 had finally arrived.

My error was never mentioned again. I was off the hook, but I had learned an extremely valuable lesson: Stay true to your core beliefs.

Things were changing at Sperry. In 1955, the company acquired Remington Rand, including its Univac division, which had produced one of the very first commercial computers in the United States, the UNIVAC mainframe computer. General Douglas MacArthur was appointed Chairman of the Board of the newly renamed Sperry Rand. I was chosen to work with General MacArthur's staff to integrate the two companies, which was now a billion dollar corporation with 80,000 employees. Working with someone from Remington, we'd begun to plan the restructuring. As a result, my life changed: I now had to commute daily by train from my home on Long Island to the Sperry Rand building, our new headquarters on Sixth Avenue, next to Radio City Music Hall.

My contact with General MacArthur was limited to a quarterly status meeting, at his suite in the Waldorf-Astoria, where he lived with his wife and son. I would meet with him in his office, an elegantly furnished room filled with memorabilia from his distinguished career as Superintendent of West Point, Chief of Staff of the U.S. Army, and Supreme

Commander of the Allied Forces in the Southwest Pacific.

Although he wore civilian clothing, we all addressed him as General MacArthur. He was very professional, and he conducted our meetings in a businesslike but relaxed manner.

During one of our meetings in 1960, General MacArthur suddenly announced that he had reset the order of Sperry Rand's priorities. "Walter," he said. "I have a more urgent job in mind for you. Our British division, Sperry Ltd., is losing millions of pounds a year. I'm appointing you acting managing director. I want you to go to London and stop the bleeding."

Coming from General MacArthur, the words sounded like an order. It was all I could do not to salute. Next stop: London.

Banking the Furnace in London

MY ENGLISH CULTURAL EDUCATION STARTED ALMOST AS SOON AS I TOUCHED down at Heathrow Airport. I was met by a man who introduced himself as Mr. Nigel, my private driver, who despite my declarations to call me Walter, cheerily refused to call me by my first name. I soon learned that people were far more formal in England than in the United States. I was never Walter, always "Mr. Scherr" to my English colleagues, and nobody at the plant was ever addressed by their first name.

Mr. Nigel took me to the Royal Garden Hotel in Kensington, right next to the beautiful park where Princess Margaret lived. The next morning, he was waiting downstairs to drive me to Sperry headquarters. Sperry Ltd, along with many of England's most important industrial companies, was located on the "Golden Mile," a section of London's Great West Road. As I stared out the window of "my" car at the great metropolis around me, I thought about the distance I had traveled from Queens to the upholstered leather back seat of a limo in London.

My first task as acting Managing Director was to meet with the company's executives. We spent several hours discussing Sperry's problems, and my goals for solving them. Then a group of my new co-workers walked me around the corner to have lunch at "the house," a much classier and more exclusive version of the typical American executive dining room. Only the top fifteen executives were allowed to eat there, and we were waited on by an all-male staff that treated us as if we were guests at a formal dinner party. After lunch, which was served on bone china, I noticed that most of the men had a glass of sherry, and quite a few stayed on to play a game of whist before they went back to work. I kept my thoughts to myself and instead of playing cards, I headed over to the factory floor to introduce myself to the plant workers.

I was always a big believer in the "walk-around" management style. I liked to walk around and talk to the employees to get a sense of how people were feeling, and whether I had to resolve any problems before they blew up into a crisis. At Sperry's Long Island facility, the factory was so huge that I usually had to ride around on one of the three-wheeled bicycles that the workers used to carry materials from the stock room to various parts of the floor. But here in London, I could stroll around the floor, introduce myself, and chat for a minute or two to ask the fellow a few questions about which machine or product he was working on. I normally enjoyed these conversations because I was genuinely curious about the production side of our business. But here in London, every one of the men I spoke to on the factory floor was so reticent; so reluctant to engage in even the most innocuous conversation, that I cut short my tour. Something was wrong. As I went back upstairs, I remembered that people in New York had warned me that the English could be very reserved. "Chilly was more like it," I thought.

I was surprised to see that all the vice presidents were gathered in my office. Before I had a chance to open my mouth, one of them spoke up. "Mr. Scherr, we're happy you're here," he said. "We're sure you're very competent, and we know we need improvement. But in England, the Managing Director doesn't go down to the floor. He talks to the vice president in charge of that function."

The other men smiled and nodded their agreement.

"I understand," I said politely.

What I really wanted to say was, "That's crazy! How the heck am I supposed to make this place profitable if I can't see with my own eyes what's happening at the factory, and talk to the people actually doing the work?"

But on further reflection, I realized what had happened: The factory workers had figured I was poking around to make sure they were doing what they were supposed to be doing. They must have sent somebody running upstairs to complain about me before I got halfway across the room.

"Stay Away from the Factory Floor!" was lesson one in the book I eventually could have written: How to Run a British Company—a Beginner's Guide for Americans. It seemed as if every day I discovered yet another difference between American and British management styles. British executives, at least those at the very top, were treated like royalty. If Mr. Nigel thought the oil in my limo needed to be changed, or its tires rotated, or its body washed and waxed, he would drop it off in the morning at the executives' on-site service center and pick it up at the end of the day. The mechanic who'd worked on it would hand over the keys and say, "Gawdon Bennet, Guv'nah!" which was Cockney for "Good as new, boss!" (Or so I thought: I have subsequently learned that it's an expression of surprise. So perhaps the mechanic was surprised that I actually thanked him for his services, which a British executive would not have done.)

Traditions, culture, established patterns of doing things—these are all fine, unless things are being done wrong. The limo, the personal driver, the private home for sumptuous meals and card games...these and the rest of the perks didn't make sense at a company that was millions of pounds in the red. A large part of the problem was the nature of the Sperry Ltd.'s contracts, almost all of which were with the British government. During the war, the government had signed a "cost plus percentage" contract. Simply put, if Sperry had a project that cost $100, it could bill the government $100 plus a negotiated percentage of the cost, which meant that Sperry always made a profit. But in the belt-tightening, post-war years, the government had switched to "fixed price" contracts, so if Sperry agreed to a fee of $100 for a project, but the actual cost added up to $105, Sperry lost money. On the other hand, if the project cost only $90 to complete, Sperry made a profit of $10. The company obviously needed to lower expenses and increase productivity. I was sure I could make that happen, but it wouldn't be easy—and it would take some time. Most of the employees had worked at Sperry since the 1940s. They were pretty stuck in their ways and resistant to any change in the status quo.

Still, I didn't want to let General MacArthur down. I needed to try and make a change in the way this company was run. After a month,

I called for an all-hands-on-deck breakfast meeting at the Hilton Hotel, Grand Ballroom.

I wanted to share with the employees what I'd observed in the month I'd been there, and what I felt needed to happen in order to turn the company around and make it profitable. But again, there was the cultural difference: I couldn't figure out how to approach and relate my findings to the employees in a memorable and meaningful way. Baseball analogies wouldn't work in a land where cricket is the national pastime. Invoking great American heroes—"here's what General MacArthur would do..."—wouldn't work either: while we were staunch allies, the Brits had their own proud military tradition. Even rolling out that paragon of great American virtue, George Washington, would have been a mistake. In their history books, George Washington was a traitorous rebel, not the father of his country. So mentioning him was out of the question, too. Gawdun Bennett, Guvnah! What was I going to do?

A few days before I was scheduled to deliver the speech, I strolled down London's Great West Road. Like the rest of London, it was covered by a thick curtain of fog. This was typical: at the time, coal was the only form of energy to heat the home and operate industry. Back in New York, I'd seen a couple of Sherlock Holmes movies. Basil Rathbone, who played the famous British sleuth, was frequently shown with his sidekick, Dr. John Watson (played by the British actor Nigel Bruce), hurrying through the streets of London, which were always thick with "pea soup fog." The thick, gloomy mist was actually created by special effects experts on a Hollywood back lot to evoke an exaggerated sense of danger. In fact, the real fog in London was frequently so dense that you couldn't see your hands in front of your face. Instead of "snow days," we had "fog days," when we had to close the plant because people couldn't find their way to work.

But that morning, as I walked along pondering my speech, the acrid smell, and thick clouds of coal smoke that filled the air brought me back not to Hollywood's depiction of London, but to an even more unlikely place: Ozone Park. I thought of the day when, at age 13, I had been given the responsibility by my dad to take over the chore known as "banking the furnace." It was this experience that led me to the most memorable speech of my career.

Banking the furnace was a rite of passage to many a 13-year-old boy in pre-war America. At that time, we all used coal for fuel. You'd store it in your basement and feed it to the furnace as needed, which in the winter was almost constantly. But coal was expensive and to burn it most efficiently required a daily "banking"—essentially, shifting the coal and dust around in order to keep the fire simmering overnight, at just the right temperature, so that you (and in our case, our tenants) didn't wake up to a freezing house. But of course you wouldn't want to burn the house down, either, so proper banking required a certain technique. It took skill, the right touch, patience—a lot of the same virtues required to run a business.

Perhaps most importantly, I thought that talking about banking the furnace would establish common ground, and help foster a sense that all of us—I, the American; the Brits; management; factory floor workers—were on the same team. This was something that seemed lacking here.

I would give my speech over lunch in the grand ballroom of the London Hilton. There were going to be about a thousand people in the audience, from all levels of management. They were from London as well as Sperry's second British plant in Southampton, where we had about ten thousand employees.

The night before, I called a meeting with my top 15 senior managers; all the whist-playing, Sherry-sipping big shots at the company. "This is what we're not going to do tomorrow," I told them. "We're not all going sit up on a dais, looking down on the rest of our co-workers. That's absolutely the wrong message. Instead, I'm going to have each of you sit at different tables." I'm sure this idea didn't sit well with all of these men, products of the English class system—you expect me to mix with the commoners?—but I didn't care. It was important, that for once, we worked like a team.

The next day, I stood up to a hushed crowd of a thousand people, most of whom had never seen, much less heard of the Yank who had come over to run their show. But instead of chastising them (as I think many expected) or giving them some Rah-Rah Win One for the Gipper speech (who?), I started by telling them about how I banked the furnace as a kid. I saw a few people taken aback, but some chuckled and others nodded their heads. "I know you're experts in coal and furnaces here in England," I said. "So tell me, what are the skills needed to bank the furnace?" Hands shot up.

"Skill."

"Perseverance."

"Determination."

"A bloody good coat, because it's cold here in winter."

We all laughed.

"And what did we fear most when it was our responsibility to bank the furnace?" I continued. "That's right...the fire going out. It was a mortal sin in my house, I can tell you that!"

Laughter.

"The old man would have tanned my hide, too, guv," called out one wag.

The ice was broken, we were starting to come together, just as I'd hoped.

"Now," I went on, "those same values, the ones you and I learned as kids, are going to apply to us here in the workplace."

I then unveiled my strategic plan, my "grand plan" as I called it, in which everyone would be involved. We were going to have goals—not 15, not 20, not different goals for different plants or divisions, but five common goals as a company. In turn, each department would have five goals that were linked to those five overarching corporate goals; and—this was important—every employee had to have one personal goal.

"From now on," I said, "if something comes up in meetings or in day-to-day situations that doesn't apply to one of those five goals, or to your specific divisional or personal goals, we don't waste time with it. It's going to make your life and mine a lot simpler."

I had to reach for one sports analogy, and with my then-limited knowledge of English sports, I tried one known the world over. "I know you're famous for your great rowing competitions at Cambridge and Oxford," I said. "We know all those teams are made up of smart, well-conditioned young men, who have practiced hard. But what does the winner do better than the rest?"

These middle management guys at Sperry Britain weren't dumb. They knew where I was going.

"They all pulled together, chief," called out someone in the audience.

"That's right. They all pulled in the same direction, they worked as a team, and they did so because they had a clear goal, just as you and I had clear goals when we were little nippers banking the furnaces in our homes."

There were chuckles at my effort to integrate a little British slang into my talk.

"Now," I concluded "we're going to do the same thing here. We're going to bank the corporate furnace by having clear goals, by using our skills, through our planning, knowledge, determination, precision, and hard work. You did it with the sifter in your hand, you can do it now."

Looking back, I guess it was a bit of a rah-rah speech after all. But I think I learned a lesson in communication about finding common ground. And in my travels around the world for various enterprises in the next few decades, it was valuable knowledge. I daresay it is today in the new, more internationalized business environment. And while I doubt the Chinese, Brazilians, Indians, or for that matter today's Brits would relate to the banking the furnace speech today, the idea behind it—finding a common theme to get all employees motivated and moving in a common direction—is still a sound one.

The speech I gave that day at the London Hilton became known in the industrial industry as "banking the furnace for profit." It has been referred to in trade and professional journals in the years since. A few months after the speech, when we had to do our periodic meeting with London's big wigs, several Lords of something or other made a point of locating me. "Are you the American that made that furnace speech?" they'd ask. "Good show!"

By now, I figured everyone in Sperry management in the U.S., from General MacArthur on down, was patting themselves on the back about how smart they'd been to send that Walter Scherr guy to London to get those Brits in shape. So a couple of months later, when I got a call from the newly-appointed president of Sperry U.S., I was sure he was coming over to marvel at what Walter had wrought, and maybe even give me a personal commendation from the General himself!

The new president was a guy named Mario and he'd replaced the man who had been in charge during the strike. Unlike that fellow, Mario was a down-to-earth guy from Brooklyn, and we had a lot in common. We both came from tight-knit families that had suffered during the Depression, and we'd grown up under difficult financial circumstances.

I'd been sending Mario monthly summaries of my progress at Sperry Ltd., as well as more detailed quarterly reports that he shared with the stockholders. But now he wanted to hear from me directly. As usual, he didn't bother to say hello or ask how I was; just got right down to business. "How's it going over there?"

I tried a little levity. "The best thing that could happen would be for this whole place to burn down," I said.

It was a moment of humor between two guys who understood each other—or so I thought. The next call I got was from Mario's secretary.

Mario would be arriving in London next week. I should arrange to have someone pick him up at the airport.

I assured her that I'd be delighted to pick him up, and could she please tell him that I looked forward to showing him some of my favorite sites in London. But when I met Mario at the gate, he wasn't his usual warm, effusive self. I was almost running out of small talk by the time we got to my gleaming black limo. Dressed as usual in his spotless uniform and cap, Mr. Nigel stood waiting for us. He opened the back door and held out his hand to take Mario's bag.

"What the hell is this?" Mario sputtered.

I almost had to shove him into the back seat. "That's the way it's done over here," I said, sliding in next to him.

Recognizing that my American boss wasn't interested in London's famous sites, Mr. Nigel kept silent during the drive from the airport. When we reached the Sperry building and Mr. Nigel jumped out to open the door for us, Mario glared at him. Professional as always, Mr. Nigel maintained his blank gaze and wished us both a good day. I hurried Mario upstairs, not stopping to make introductions. We got right down to work and spent the next few hours reviewing all the figures I'd put together, along with my forecasts and estimated profit and loss statements for the next six months.

When Mario finally decided he was ready to eat lunch, I told him we were going over to the executive dining room. I figured that once he saw the house, he would begin to understand that the divide between Sperry Gyroscope on Long Island and British Sperry in London was as wide as the Atlantic Ocean. He had plenty of questions for me about the data we'd just reviewed, but the moment we stepped into the dining room, he closed up like a clam. I'd seen Mario get angry a few times, and his explosions always reminded me of a summer afternoon when I was driving somewhere out west. I noticed the storm clouds first, gathering far in the distance, and then I saw the downpour coming in my direction. I knew I should find some place safe, away from the wind and lightning and hail, but I just stayed in my car and drove toward it.

As I brought him over to a table to join several of our vice presidents, I suddenly thought about that storm. I wished I'd explained to him that the British were a lot more understated than the people he and I had grown up with in New York. But as I was about to introduce him, the Vice President of Manufacturing, who was seated next to me, off handedly announced to the chief engineer, "The blokes in the machine shop went out on strike today."

This was the first I'd heard of a strike. I was sure Mario's reaction was the same as mine: I should know about everything that was going on at the plant. I didn't want any surprises, especially when I was sitting next to the person I reported to, who'd flown to London specifically to discuss the company's financial future.

Mario elbowed me in the ribs so hard I was sure at least one of them was cracked, maybe even broken. My judgment was so clouded by pain that I had the crazy notion I could warn the vice president to change the story so that it made more sense. "Why didn't you tell me?" I asked.

"Mr. Scherr, you have so much on your plate that I didn't want to burden you with another problem. Besides, I was sure the blokes would come back at the end of the day."

The poor guy. He had dug himself into a hole so deep he could have been buried in it standing up. I tensed up, expecting another elbow in my ribs.

Mario pushed back his chair. "Into the kitchen!" he barked at me. Hoping to prevent a full-scale explosion, I hurried after him, but he was already screaming at the workers as I rushed into the kitchen. "All of you! Get out of here now!"

Frozen with fear, the cooks and dishwashers stared at the red-faced maniac who had burst into their space.

"Can't you understand English? Get out of here now!"

In fact, many of them couldn't understand much English, and Mario's rage-inflected Brooklyn accent was especially hard for them to decipher.

Still screaming, he began to pound on the counter, which propelled the workers into motion. I felt as if I were in the middle of a Marx Brothers movie. The cooks flung down their ladles and spatulas, the waiters let go of trays full of food, the dishwashers dropped wet silverware and plates all over the floor. Dishes flew in every direction. Shards of china and glass crunched under foot. The staff fled en masse, shoving their way through the door that connected the kitchen with the dining room.

Feeling anything but calm, I took a deep breath, stared at Mario without blinking, and said, "Your behavior is upsetting a whole lot of people. You have to stop screaming. Now."

He tried to interrupt me, but I kept on talking. "You sent me over here to do a job, and I've already managed to cut our losses. Can

I make this place profitable? I don't know yet, but I'm making every effort to do so, I do know that management is now on the same page, and we have clearly defined goals. But it's not going to happen overnight, and it's certainly not going to happen any faster with you screaming at them or me."

Mario was an emotional guy with an explosive temper, but he also knew when to keep quiet and listen. In many ways we spoke the same language. He listened as I fast-talked my way through a summary of the previous three months. I told him about the difference in culture, about how the stratified class system of English society at that time applied in the factory as well, where management and workers didn't mix and mingle. I even told him about the banking of the furnace speech, and as I gathered he'd had to tend many a coal fire in his family's apartment in Brooklyn during cold Depression-era nights, I could see that he understood the comparison. He may have even smiled. But by the time the staff began to make their way timidly back into the kitchen, he was calm, and had a much better feeling about what was happening on the other side of the Pond.

Mario probably set a record for shortest trip by an American CEO to London: He left that night. By the time he departed, he seemed satisfied that I knew what I was doing. That didn't mean we should tolerate strikes, but unions had a kind of clout in England at that time that we couldn't imagine here, and a management culture that was elitist and certainly didn't help the situation. Still, the easier interaction between management and staff that happened in many American corporations was never going to be the norm here, at least not in that era. We had to accommodate our employees' customs, as long as they didn't interfere with our production schedules and the bottom line.

One of those English rituals was teatime, which took place promptly at 2:30 every afternoon. Heaven help us Americans if we tried to change any part of that tradition. Another tradition in which I had to participate was the managing director's annual visit to "the City," London's equivalent of Wall Street. Four times a year, all the top executives who worked for the large industrial companies on the Great West Road got dressed up in tails and top hats to meet with government officials. Our discussions ranged from politics, the economy, recent governmental rulings, and whatever other topics anyone cared to raise. Including, as I've mentioned, my banking the furnace speech.

During one of our meetings, we spent much of the time talking about coal heat again. But this time it wasn't related to the speech. The coal-fueled fog that had inspired my idea for that speech was a serious health hazard. So many people suffered from lung disease and other respiratory conditions. As a former TB patient, that certainly touched me; I hated to see people, especially children, afflicted with these kinds of breathing ailments.

The English government had been developing new towns outside of London to help reduce the city's overcrowded neighborhoods, antiquated housing, and pollution. Making these communities viable required jobs, which in turn required the presence of large employers. We were one of them. To persuade us to leave the Great West Road, the government offered Sperry and other neighboring businesses excellent financial packages: all our expenses paid for the first year; tax relief for ten years; and money to relocate employees and train new staff. Sperry Ltd. would move to Bracknell, thirty miles west of downtown London, where homes were being built for twenty-five thousand people. I was also given the chance to make a fresh start. We could decide which of our employees should be encouraged to relocate to the new facility—and to new homes—in Bracknell.

During my first year in England, we had reduced our losses from previous years by one-third, but we still had a long way to go. Whether it was fate or the English government, I believed that the move to Bracknell would enable British Sperry to become profitable within a three-year period. I presented the proposed changes to Sperry's Board of Directors in New York. I committed to extending my involvement with Sperry Ltd. for three more years. I would continue to serve as acting Managing Director for one more year, and I would find my replacement, who would begin serving as managing director during the second year. And I would commute between New York and England for the third year. The Board approved my proposal, so on to Bracknell it was.

Although relocating the plant was an immense undertaking, I found time to relax with new friends who showed me how the British spent their nonworking hours. I discovered that their loyalties were first to Queen and country, then to their families, and third to cricket, which was played on every pitch in every community on Sundays.

At first resistant to participate, I'd finally acceded to demands from friends and neighbors to "give it a bloody go." When I did, the results were surprising. "Hey, Yank," I heard more than once, "how'd you get so good at this game?" I'd tell them that cricket was similar to stickball, a game they'd never heard of, but which they found fascinating, particularly the way we measured hits in terms of sewer lengths.

In my few spare hours, I learned to love yet another seemingly arcane but quintessentially English pastime: lawn bowling. I'd found a pub near my flat where I'd often go after work for a beer and a sandwich. After a while, I got to be friends with some of the other regulars, who always seemed to be chatting about lawn bowling. When I asked them how it was played, one of the fellows said I should come by one Saturday and see what was going on. Watching them on the field, alternately encouraging and insulting one another, they reminded me about my pals in Ozone Park, and I got a little nostalgic and home-sick. My pub friends must have understood, because the next time I showed up for a beer, they invited me to join their team. Most of the pubs had their own lawn bowling team, each one with its own col-ors and cheerleaders. Nobody cared where you worked or what you did, as long as you gave everything for your team during the weekly Saturday matches.

My team had one advantage over the rest of the fellows: we traveled in style. Dressed in our colors, we'd all pile into the limo, and Mr. Nigel would drive us to wherever we were playing that day. Most of my teammates had never ridden in a limo, and it was a terrific thrill for them. We all felt like stars, and our opponents didn't know what to make of our very unusual mode of transportation.

Had you told me over a pint after lawn bowling one weekend that I would soon be leaving both London and Sperry, where I'd worked now for 13 years, I would have dismissed it.

I had learned a lot about business since my release from Otisville. I'd learned that, whether it's Sperry or Henry and Fritz's luncheonette on Liberty Avenue, you have to maintain a balance among the same three constituents: the employees, the customers, and the stockholders. If you give dividends in excess to the company's profits, the customers and the employees suffer. If you give too much to the customers, you damage your relationship with the employees and the stockholders. If you pay your employees a salary that's not commensurate with industry standards, you hurt your stockholders and customers.

Often through hard experience, I had also learned the "how to's" of being a corporate leader: managing a department; treating employees with respect; setting up standards and goals; finding a way to deliver the product as promised; and maintaining a profitable bottom line.

The company invested in me, and I gave them a return on their investment. It was a win-win for both sides. Why, I would have thought at the time, should I ever walk away from this?

The answer: only when an extraordinary opportunity presented itself, which it soon did.

TEX AND TERESA

During the three years I was in charge of British Sperry, I made a lot of new friends from both sides of the Atlantic. My new acquaintances were a disparate group: from Cockney pub mates and lawn bowling teammates to executives who, like me, represented American corporations. Some of my best times amongst this group were spent with people from Litton Industries.

While not as well remembered today as they should be, everybody knew Litton back then, and not just because it was a huge, multinational corporation. Litton generated what we'd call today "buzz" in the business world, largely through its colorful, brilliant co-founder Charles B. "Tex" Thornton, Jr.

Thornton was indeed a native of the Lone Star State and he had a past befitting his pedigree. His father, Tex Sr., was a roughneck legend, famous for fighting oil well fires in the Texas Boom days.

Tex, Jr. became the man of the family at a young age, and soon demonstrated a business acumen that would eventually propel him into positions of enormous influence. Though he started out as a lowly clerk in the U.S. Interior Department, he had a genius for numbers, and used it to devise modern management systems, first for the Army Air Corps (the World War II precursor to the United States Air Force) and later as the founder of his own company.

During the war, Tex—who was only 28 years old at the time of Pearl Harbor—had been one of the so-called "Whiz Kids" credited with organizing a "statistical control" system that kept our air force, then fighting on numerous fronts all over the world, running efficiently. The group operated out of Harvard, adding to its mystique, and produced a number of men who would be influential in reshaping post-war America, including Robert McNamara, later the Secretary of Defense.

After the war, Henry Ford II hired the Whiz Kids, led by Thornton, to apply his methods to Ford Motor Company. When asked about this vaunted statistical control that was revolutionizing American management, he'd just chuckle, and in his best "aw shucks" drawl, dismiss it as a "fancy name for finding out what the hell we had by way of resources and when and where it was going to be required."

Soon, Tex moved on to Hughes—where he helped increase sales by $50 million in just a few years, but left because he didn't like dealing with the company's cantankerous (and later, certifiable) founder Howard Hughes. At that point, he sought out an old Whiz Kid buddy, Roy Ash, and in 1953, they started their own company, Electro Dynamics Corporation. Within a year they bought out a company that manufactured vacuum tubes and set out to make their new venture, Litton Industries, a major player in the Cold War world—and beyond. When he went to Lehman Brothers to help fund his new enterprise, Tex painted a futuristic picture of Litton as a company positioned to flourish in the technological and scientific era he predicted America was entering.

Tex's vision proved to be uncannily accurate. In Litton, Tex was creating what would become one of the first major players in what we now call the "high tech" industry—even though today he rarely gets credit for that.

I knew all about Litton and Tex Thornton, as did any ambitious young businessman at the time. So imagine my reaction when, over dinner in London one evening in the 1960s with a group of Litton men, one of them mentioned that Tex had not only read but was a big fan of my "banking the furnace for profit" speech. I almost choked on my shepherd's pie! They went on to say that I had an open invitation to visit Litton's headquarters in Beverly Hills. Tex would be happy to meet me, they said, and they were sure that the company would be a great fit for me.

I would have signed up then and there except for one thing. Litton was headquartered in California and at that point, the last thing I was thinking about was another move. After three years spent living in England and commuting back to New York, I needed to take some vacation time, become a full-time father and husband again, and contemplate my future.

And despite my enthusiasm for Tex Thornton and the new world he was helping to invent at Litton, I felt a deep sense of loyalty to the first and only company that had hired me. Sperry had taken a chance on me when I'd had little to offer except my willingness to work hard and to learn as much as they were willing to teach me.

I was grateful to Sperry, I was proud of my association with Sperry, I counted many Sperry colleagues among my closest friends.

Still, in my heart, I realized it was time to leave.

I wanted a different kind of company. I wanted to work for people like Tex Thornton and Roy Ash who believed in expanding their company by acquiring other businesses that fit their corporate profile; people who, it is particularly clear in retrospect, were helping to change American industry.

I imagined myself as a Litton man, and I liked the picture I saw in my mind's eye.

A few months after I'd returned home, I phoned one of the Litton guys I'd met in England and told him I was interested in exploring the opportunity that had been dangled before me. He called back to say that Tex wanted to meet me in Los Angeles the following week. The company's headquarters were located in the heart of Beverly Hills. After spending so many years at Sperry's plant in the mostly blue-collar neighborhood of Lake Success—and having grown up in a modest Queens neighborhood myself—I was completely unprepared for the opulence of the surroundings, not to mention Litton's property.

Jules Stein, the founder of MCA—for many years Hollywood's reigning talent agency—had commissioned the designs for the main building, the surrounding structures, and the almost three acres of immaculately manicured grounds in the late 1930s. Stein wanted to both impress and welcome his Hollywood clients. He succeeded on both counts.

Litton had bought the English Georgian-style building from MCA in 1964. The property, which had been designed by Paul R. Williams, "architect to the stars," included a vast courtyard, carefully tended gardens, fountains, imposing statues, and a cupola. It was often referred to as "Tara," because it resembled Scarlett O'Hara's plantation home in *Gone with the Wind*. Stepping onto the portico with its four classical columns, I had to stifle a laugh, thinking about what my Ozone Park buddies, not to mention my Long Island Sperry friends, would have thought of their old friend Walter Scherr—a man who would never be confused with Clark Gable—in Hollywood, walking up a staircase that looked like the one where Gable himself, as Rhett Butler, and Vivian Leigh had played out their torrid, but ill-fated Civil War romance.

At the top of the stairs, Tex and Roy were waiting for me. I liked both of them right away. Tex was smart and personable. I remember thinking that he looked like he would have made a good halfback at TCU or Texas A&M—a guy with speed and agility, who could elude tacklers, but was still strong enough to pound through an obstacle. He flattered me by mentioning how much he liked my "banking the furnace for profit" speech.

I realized that I didn't have to sell myself to the Litton folks. Over the next few days, I was wined, dined, and wooed as ardently as the young men of Clayton County had wooed Scarlett O'Hara.

Best of all, I got to listen to Tex's ideas, and it was like attending a management seminar, delivered by a folksy genius. "Walter," he'd say, "you can't win a ball game with only a pitcher and catcher, and you can't have a strong company unless it's balanced."

By the time I left Beverly Hills, I'd accepted their offer of Group Financial Vice President, responsible for seven divisions located all over the United States. I had brought up my concerns over relocation, and was reassured that I would stay in New York if I wished. Despite the allure of Southern California, Vera and I wanted to remain in Northport, where we had now planted roots: Our kids were involved in Little League and other youth activities, and Vera and I were very active in our local church.

Litton also offered me a benefits package with stock options that would one day be worth far more than I would ever have imagined.

Before I could accept their offer, however, I had to ask Sperry's board chairman if they could match it. Although I'd made up my mind to leave, it was still hard to hear the president say, "You've done a hell of a job at Sperry. We'll miss you, but we can't afford you."

I appreciated his honesty. I'd had a wonderful run there. But I was restless and eager to prove myself on a bigger playing field. It was time to move on. Litton seemed like the perfect situation to begin the next phase of my life—and all too briefly, it was.

A few weeks after I'd started working at Litton, Tex's secretary called to tell me I needed to come out to Beverly Hills immediately for an urgent meeting. She hung up before I had a chance to ask any questions. An hour later, another secretary called to say that my round-trip ticket would be waiting for me at the JFK first-class check-in counter. That's how it was done at Litton: We were expected to produce results, but we were treated well.

Arriving at Tara, I still felt as if I didn't belong at a company that occupied such an exquisite setting. My mood changed as soon as I entered the second floor meeting room and Tex introduced me to the two grim-faced men seated alongside him at the conference table: one of them, a former FBI agent, was now Litton's vice president of Security;

the other was the vice president in charge of Litton's Washington office. I reassured myself that I hadn't worked at Litton long enough to commit any crimes. Why was I there?

Tex quickly gave me the answer. A group of congressmen had accused Litton of overcharging the Pentagon by several million dollars for electronic equipment and spare parts. They were on the verge of calling a congressional investigation that could seriously damage Litton's position as one of the country's leading military defense contractors. Even a whiff of such misconduct could send the company's stock spiraling downward. Tex and Roy had built Litton into one of the hottest companies listed on the New York Stock Exchange. There was a lot to lose here. Tex believed in the honesty of his employees, but he needed to find out whether even a shred of evidence existed to support the congressmen's claims.

Because of my accounting background, Tex realized that I would know where to look and what questions to ask in an internal audit. He suspected that a flaw in Litton's accounting system might have caused the financial discrepancies the congressmen claimed to have uncovered. I agreed with his theory.

Let me cut to the chase: It turned out that Tex and I were right. The problem was no more than a glitch in Litton's accounting system. There would be no congressional inquiry, no scandal—at least not then. But the release of tension, the collective sigh of relief not only in Litton, but on Wall Street and probably in some quarters of Washington, D.C. when this was announced, was palpable and revealing. The last thing anybody wanted was the Head Whiz Kid and his hot-stock company-of-the-future collapsing in scandal.

Least of all, their most recent hire: me!

I moved on to my next project—and this was right in Litton's sweet spot: a new technology, although I must admit that when I first heard about it, I thought they were joking.

I was told that we had exclusive worldwide rights to distribute a new machine that, using telephone lines, could somehow transmit a newspaper's page layouts from an editor's office to the printing plant.

"What?" I said when this was first explained to me in a meeting. "You're telling me that the editor of the Daily News in midtown Manhattan could somehow send his layouts to the printing plant in Long Island City or wherever...through his telephone?"

Exactly right. "Well, does this thing have a name?" I asked.

I was told that it was called a "Press Fax" machine.

Short for "facsimile," the technology had, in various and more primitive forms, been around for decades.

Just a couple of years earlier, Xerox had introduced a device that could connect to a phone line and transmit a letter-sized document in about six minutes.

These were the precursors to the modern fax machine. The Press Fax was larger than what would eventually become the standard home or office version. It required different toner and larger paper, but it was already being used by many newspapers overseas. And in Japan, where there were already about sixty thousand of these machines in use—forty thousand of these Press Fax machines were built by a subsidiary of the Matsushita Corporation—they'd already moved beyond newspapers. The Japanese were using them to transmit bank documents and make transactions; railroads used it as a form of instant communication.

These large, complicated machines used Japanese characters, of course, and bore little resemblance to the fax you can still buy for $99 in your local consumer electronics store. Still, the growing use of facsimile in Japan at this early date already hinted at the potential of what would become one of the most important new communications technologies of the next decade.

The Japanese were far ahead of us, clearly, and many American companies had approached Matsushita about producing the machines for the Western market. Their overtures were rejected. The giant Japanese corporation was, however, ready to deliver about a million dollars' worth of these Press Fax machines to Litton.

"What?" I said, sitting up straight, when I heard this. "A million dollar purchase of a product that no one here has even heard of, much less approved?"

In fact, nobody at Litton had authorized such a purchase, nor did we intend to buy the machines at that point. The whole thing had been a miscommunication between Matsushita and one of our vice presidents during a trip to Japan.

It was, as Tex diplomatically framed it, "a very delicate situation." Matsushita produced millions of dollars of business equipment for Litton, and the two companies had an excellent relationship, no small thing to the Japanese. My job was to preserve our reputation and resolve this colossal misunderstanding.

To navigate my way through Japanese business culture, I chose Frank DiSanto, the chief engineer in my group. Frank, who had been to

Japan many times, would be my guide. He was also great company. As we flew across the Pacific, he did his best to educate me in the intricacies of Japanese etiquette. "Don't forget, Walter," he said. "When they're nodding that means they understand. It doesn't necessarily mean they agree."

I nodded.

At Matsushita's headquarters in Tokyo, we were ushered into a room that was crowded with about twenty executives and translators. As we were welcomed, introduced, and offered tea, I told myself that Tex and Roy were depending on me. And if I seemed to be going too far wrong, I figured that Frank could step in to save me. I silently offered a quick prayer for help, took a deep breath, and addressed the Matsushita executives.

"As you know, I'm in charge of the division now," I said. "I've reviewed all the paperwork with our lawyers, and I'm sorry to say that Litton has no legal obligation to pay for those machines."

Whoosh!

The moment that translator had interpreted those words, you could almost hear the sound; as if all the air had just gone out of the room. Matsushita had millions of dollars in inventory tied up in those machines. I didn't need a translator to tell me how upset they were. I quickly explained that Litton's goal was to help both our companies make the best of a bad situation. But first, I explained, Frank and I needed to do an inventory at their factory.

We had to figure out the number of equivalent units in production at the factory. In other words, how many of the machines were finished and ready to ship? How many were almost completed? How many were in the early stage of production?

Frank and I spent the next week at their factory, walking around the floor, inspecting the assembly lines, and taking notes on all the parts. In the evenings, we took long walks through Tokyo. After the fire-bombings of World War II, the city had been rebuilt into a densely popu-lated patchwork of private homes with family-run businesses on the first floor and many beautiful public gardens, parks, and temples. The streets were narrow and crowded, but everyone was courteous. People always stopped to give us directions; they would go out of their way to take us wherever we were headed.

Sunday was family day, and the parks were filled with people. Ev-erywhere we looked, children were running and jumping and skipping. They stood still only long enough to stare at us. The American occupation of Japan had ended in 1952; thirteen years later, tall white men were rela-tively exotic, and we might have been the first Caucasians these youngsters had ever seen. Everywhere we went, people wanted to take pictures of us.

As we posed and smiled, I thought about what a remarkable transition this country had made in such a relatively short time. Some of the credit had to go to my old boss Douglas MacArthur. The same man who'd sent me to London had spent the years after the war presiding over the Japanese Occupation and helping to guide the defeated nation toward a democratic system of government, which many believe helped lay the groundwork for what would become known as the Japanese Mir-acle—its re-emergence as an economic superpower.

I was witnessing that miracle every day.

One memorable evening, Frank and I were invited to join sev-eral of Matsushita's top people at a geisha house. Foreigners were rarely allowed into the Japanese equivalent of a gentleman's exclusive private club, so receiving an invitation was a show of respect for my position.

Westerners often mistake geishas for high-priced prostitutes who worked behind the closed doors of the geisha houses. That's not true: these were an elite group of women who had spent years learning to perform traditional Japanese dance and music, to make conversation or flirt, to provide sympathy or humor, depending on their client's mood. An experienced geisha was the perfect hostess, providing companionship, entertainment, food, wine, tea—whatever he desired.

When the geishas discovered that I was the youngest man in our group, they assigned the youngest geisha, nicknamed "Baby," to be my companion for the evening. Sitting cross-legged on the floor next to a beautiful young woman whose sole responsibility was to cater to all my whims, I flashed back to the awkward, shy young man from Queens who had had his first date with a woman at age 28.

The inevitable, recurring question echoed in my brain:

How in the world did I get here?

The negotiations took considerable time and creative thinking, but in the end we reached an understanding: Matsushita agreed to stop producing new parts and machines for Litton; Litton committed to buying ten machines from Matsushita that were close to completion.

We left Japan with our reputation intact and on good terms with Matsushita. I didn't get to spend much time at home, however, because now I had to find buyers for these big Press Fax machines. My goal—to sell all ten within a two- to three-month period—required a first-rate sales team and a willingness to put in a lot of miles.

I chose Jim McCarthy, a Litton vice president of sales with thirty-plus years' experience in telecommunication equipment, to take charge of marketing our machines in England and other European countries. Jim had spent twenty years selling business equipment overseas. Charming and conscientious, with a great sense of humor, Jim was the consummate salesman with contacts throughout Europe. When he assured me he could find buyers for six machines, I had every reason to believe him.

I handpicked three salesmen to work with me in Saudi Arabia, Kuwait, and India.

My trip there was one of the most memorable in a lifetime of travel. I will never forget my first impression of Delhi—the smell of spices, an overpowering mixture that was totally foreign to me. Then the crowded streets that throbbed with the throngs of people pressing in on me: walking, running, crawling, all of them competing for space with the legions of bicycles, rickshaws, handcarts, oxcarts, buses, and cars. And the animals—cats, dogs, monkeys, goats, and oxen—so many species navigating the same thoroughfares but all headed in different directions. Traffic lights were nonexistent, and the traffic signs and lines on the roads seemed to be suggestions that everyone ignored. The noise was all-encompassing and overwhelming. The sounds I heard in India were the sounds of life, the heartbeat of five thousand years.

I learned by trial and error—mostly error—how to deal with government agencies and the bureaucrats who ran them. In those years, India was still very much a hybrid of Asian traditions and British colonial rule, even though it had achieved independence in 1947. When I arrived there, I knew nothing about how to negotiate the system.

During the weeks I spent in India, I got to know Mr. Patel, Litton's distributor, and my own personal expert on all things Indian, who invited me to his home for dinner to meet his family. Like many visitors, I was struck by the enormous disparity in living conditions between an upper-middle-class family like the Patel's, and the people I saw living on the street just a few blocks away from his spacious, beautifully decorated house. During dinner, a mini-banquet of spicy vegetarian food, he explained that according to Hinduism, India's major religion, when people die, their physical bodies die, as well. But their souls live on forever through the process of reincarnation: a continuous cycle of birth, death, and rebirth. Their karma—their destiny and their future—depends on how they conducted themselves in their previous lives.

While these have become well-understood concepts and terms in the West, this was the first time I'd heard any of it. Our family priest, Father Jolly, never talked about karma or reincarnation. While it didn't quite fit into my understanding of Catholic theology, it was fascinating nonetheless.

By way of explanation, Mr. Patel said that in a previous life, he had been a very poor person. But he had worked very hard and therefore his karma was to come back as a distributor for Litton, a person who could afford a very fine house, a cook and several other servants, and delicious food.

I would have loved to have posed questions about the meaning of life to the most famous person I met in India.

Born in Albania with the unpronounceable name of Anjeze Gonxhe Bojaxhiu, she had left her native land at age 18 to pursue the life of a missionary. She worked and studied in Ireland, before arriving in Calcutta, where she took her vows in 1931. She founded the Missionaries of Charity, a congregation of nuns dedicated to serving the poor, disabled, sick, and dying, "...all those people who feel...uncared for throughout society, people that have become a burden to the society and are shunned by everyone."

By the time I met her, she was known to all by her religious name, Teresa. Mother Teresa.

Let me emphasize that I didn't have a meeting with Mother Teresa to discuss fax machines or the weather or even reincarnation. Indeed, I didn't even have a one-on-one conversation with her. But I was privileged enough to be among an audience of about 35 foreign business executives that got to hear her speak one evening about her work at the Kalighat Home for the Dying, the hospice she had established in Calcutta.

She was short and frail looking, but greeted us warmly, grasping each of our outstretched hands with both of hers. And I still remember one of the things she told us that night.

"You don't have to always succeed, but you have to try," she said. "God wants you to try."

Hearing Mother Teresa speak was one of the great privileges of my life—and a turning point. Like many of her patients, I had been shunned because I had been poor and very ill. The men who had cared for me at Otisville had been anything but saintly; I doubt that many of them even believed in God. But thanks to their support and attention, I had survived, and now my mission was clear. I left India knowing that whatever else I did with my life, I would find a way to recognize and reward those who devoted themselves to caring for other human beings, regardless of who they were.

This book, in fact, is a continuation of that very mission; one inspired by the words of a tiny, frail-looking woman, spoken nearly a half century ago.

I left India with my mind and senses reeling. I had sold two of our six fax machines in India, and I had two more to unload in Saudi Arabia and Kuwait. I'm sure I could have found fascinating places and people there, but what I needed most was calm and quiet after the sensory overload of India. Litton's representative in Saudi Arabia had made appointments with his key accounts. I was so ready to be back in New York that I hardly even left my hotel in Riyadh, except to meet with the companies that had expressed interest in the fax machines. In two weeks, we sold the last two machines.

The trip was a success, and Tex and Roy were delighted with the way we'd straightened out the debacle. But Frank and I saw something else that was even more important; we were convinced that a market for a general-purpose facsimile existed in the United States. We'd witnessed the Japanese facsimile machines transmitting information between banks branches and railroad stations. This technology was bigger than newspaper layouts. This was a potential game-changer. Those other countries recognized it; potential competitors like Xerox probably recognized it; so should we.

One evening, as I was in the middle of writing a proposal to present to Tex about how Litton could dominate the emerging communications market by developing a Western-style fax machine, my phone rang. Tex was on the other end, but before I could even say, "Hello, how are you?" he said, "We have a meeting tomorrow at two p.m." He hung up without saying goodbye.

This was uncharacteristic of Tex, but I shrugged off any worries and went upstairs to pack.

I arrived at Tara fifteen minutes before the meeting and joined a group of vice presidents who had all received the same curt phone call from Tex. We were joined in the conference room by the board members and very top executives.

At exactly two o'clock, Tex and Roy walked into the room. Tex was very somber, and Roy looked as if he hadn't slept all night.

"Litton is about to release this to the press, and we wanted you to hear it first from us. I'm sorry, but we're not taking any questions," said Tex.

The statement he read said that evidence of serious fraud had been discovered in Litton's Business Equipment Group. A number of Litton executives were involved in giving out machines on a consignment basis, but had deliberately recorded them as sales, instead. This artificially increased the company's profits and thus the price of its stock (many shares of which these executives owned).

This time there was no accounting error to blame. This was a crime—and Litton was fully committed to prosecuting the people involved.

After Tex read the statement, the room was hushed. Wall Street's reaction was anything but. "Savage and quick" was how one commentator described the impact that news of the scandal had on Litton's once-vaunted stock. After 57 consecutive quarters of earnings increases Litton suffered its first earnings decline—and it was a whopper: Earnings fell to $7.2 million for the 2nd quarter of fiscal year 1968 with earnings per share of 21 cents—a 30 percent drop from year earlier earnings of $16 million or 63 cents a share.

Although it would take years, Litton would rebound eventually, and in 2001 would be sold to Northrup-Grumman. But great damage to its prestige and reputation was done that day in 1968.

I often wonder if Tex—who died in 1981—ever really recovered from the scandal. Imagine the sense of betrayal: Several of your own top executives, guys you might have known for years, essentially stabbing you in the back. Neither the fact that Litton itself, not an outside auditor, had discovered the fraud, nor the fact that the men were prosecuted and sent to jail, seemed to matter.

Like most everyone else at Litton, I took a huge hit, as well. Almost overnight, the stock that was going to make me a millionaire went spiraling downward. I didn't know how far it would fall, but I was sure it would never recover its former strength.

The scandal drained the energy, the creative juices of Litton too. All its resources had to be directed toward recovery. This was certainly not the time to be launching a new technology. Litton signed a release that relinquished to Frank and me all rights to produce and market a business fax machine.

In barely two years, and over the course of just a few days, the vision of myself as a Litton man had faded to black.

It was time to move on.

A NEW VISION

HERE'S HOW FAST AND HOW FAR WE'VE COME: TODAY, 37 PERCENT OF THE world's population—that's two-and-a-half billion people!—use the Internet, and eight more people log on every second of the day. But less than fifty years ago, people on Wall Street—the people we needed to invest in our company—didn't even understand what a fax machine was.

I know, because it was my job to explain it to them.

Now on our own, set adrift from Litton, Frank and I had spent six months creating a very detailed plan for our new business, which we called Visual Sciences. We tried to anticipate every question that might come up in a meeting, every point that had to be addressed. We worked well together; I brought my corporate experience, financial background, and my understanding of Matsushita's business methods. Frank was smart and practical. He understood exactly the mechanics of the machines, their capacities, and potential. Planning was my strong suit.

We had to have a well-crafted, persuasive presentation to get what we needed, which was seed money, any amount that would allow us to pay Matsushita to produce prototypes while enabling us to retain ownership of the drawings and toolings needed for the new fax machines.

Thus began my experience with Wall Street—or the "begging for dollars" phase of my life.

To get the kind of money we'd need to really launch this venture, I'd have to deal with a sector of society I didn't know well: The blue bloods, the elite, the guys who lived in upper-class Westchester County enclaves like Scarsdale and Larchmont and spent weekends at the same country clubs—while I was commuting home to blue-collar Northport on Long Island and watching my kids play CYO basketball.

Despite my extensive contacts in the defense and high-tech world, I had no network to tap when it came to reaching these people. But I had learned as a Long Island Press paperboy that making cold calls was essential to generating new business—no matter what business you're in. I'd refined that lesson at Sperry and most recently at Litton, where I made some very cold calls to people who didn't even speak my language.

Whenever I picked up the phone to call someone I'd never met, I reminded myself that he or she had as much to gain as I did. I also knew how to connect with people. And as the days turned into weeks as I took my dog-and-pony show around Wall Street, looking for brokers and investors willing to take a shot on two guys with one big idea, I learned even more the fine art of schmoozing, a wonderful Yiddish word for chatting, often in order to create a connection or promote a business favor.

Boy, did I schmooze! I realized that despite my lack of a pedigree, despite the fact that I'd gone to city colleges while they'd been to the Ivy League, I had something to offer to even the very WASP-y brokers on the other side of the desk: Information.

Wall Street thrived on it, and through my international experiences at Sperry and Litton, I'd accumulated some valuable insights and knowledge. As time went on, I didn't get a commitment, but I did get the sense that some of these brokers were starting to listen to me. And while we didn't call it "networking" in the early 1970s, I never left a meeting without getting a few more names to contact—and the hope that the broker I'd cold-called, and now struck up a relationship with, might remember to mention my name to someone else.

Still, I waited in vain to hear the word I wanted to hear: Yes.

In spite of our carefully drawn diagrams and pages of data about the growing market for faxes, how they worked, why they were the next "big thing" in communications, I kept hearing the same question day after day, meeting after meeting:

"What's a fax machine?"

I would try to explain that it was a long-distance version of the universally accepted photocopy machine, which was by then already a fixture in most offices. "So imagine making a copy on a photocopy machine," I would say, "except that when you fax it, the copy can emerge from someone's machine on the other side of the world."

Occasionally, someone would register a glimmer of excitement...a sort of "a-ha" moment when they realized the potential of what I was talking about. But while a few might have had the vision, they didn't have the nerve to pull the trigger. I'd walk out without a deal—again.

Cold calling without effect is draining, depressing. I'd often return home to Long Island feeling frustrated. Then I'd walk into our house, and

Vera would have a smile and a story for me, and my four children would clamor for attention. There was no time for pouting. There were Little League games to attend, church fund-raisers that had to be organized, social events to plan. We were part of an extended family: Vera's sister and her husband lived next door, and their five children were about the same age as ours. Every Sunday my parents took the train from Queens, and after church we'd all have dinner together. It reminded me of the Sundays spent at Grandma McCue's, and the lesson I'd learned in those days, which was that nothing is more important than getting together with family and friends. The menu was no longer all potatoes, all the time. But the spirit remained the same: lots of love, laughter, and storytelling.

Finally, after months of fruitless presentations, often three a day, I got a lead on a possible source for seed capital. I was having lunch with a broker from Lehman Brothers. Lehman had backed Litton when they first started a decade earlier, and this guy was smart enough to know that when someone from Litton—even, as in our case, "formerly" from Litton—had an idea it was worth listening to.

The deal was too small for Lehman, but this broker said he did know someone who might be interested: an officer of the Bank Mees and Hope, a major financial institution in the Netherlands. They had expressed an interest in investing in a small communication company in the United States.

"Hey, that's us!" I told the broker. "When can I see these people? Sooner the better!"

One week later, I was in Amsterdam, making our presentation to a Mees and Hope bank official. No translators needed here; like seemingly everyone else in his country, he spoke English fluently. He nodded at the end of my pitch. "I am interested," he said. And to my surprise, he made a more tangible demonstration of that interest. "Mr. Scherr," he said. "I am authorized by the bank to invest $600,000 in the stock transaction."

He then wrote a letter to Mees and Hope's bank in New York, Morgan Stanley, authorizing them to write a check for $600,000 upon receipt of a stock certificate from Visual Sciences for 120,000 shares.

Back in New York, we completed this transaction in less than 10 minutes. "What a difference from the painstaking negotiations with the Japanese!" I thought.

Once the transaction was complete, I immediately flew to Japan to sign a contract with Matsushita Graphic Communications, Inc. who agreed to manufacture a business facsimile machine in accordance with Visual Sciences' specifications. We owned the tooling and the drawings and had exclusive rights to sell new business facsimile equipment outside of Asia. In addition, Visual Sciences was to receive two prototypes for demonstration purposes. The cost? One hundred and fifty thousand dollars, which left us $450k to continue building the company and expand.

Thoroughly jet-lagged by now, I returned to New York energized. After more than a year, things had taken a turn for the better.

Or so it appeared.

Ten days after returning from Japan, I received a long-distance call from Amsterdam. It was the president of the Mees and Hope bank that had funded us $600,000. He spoke English too, but this was not a friendly conversation. "You have committed a fraud upon this bank!" he said.

I was dumbstruck. I tried telling him that I had met with one of his officers in Amsterdam who okayed the deal.

"He was not authorized to commit the funds and has been dismissed from the firm," said the bank president icily.

I explained to him that there was no way I could have known this. The man I had met with seemed to have all the proper paperwork and credentials. What was I supposed to do, I asked, give him a lie detector test before I accepted his offer to save my fledgling business? Besides, I continued, "we've spent a hundred and fifty thousand dollars on tooling drawings, prototypes, and exclusive worldwide rights to sell the machines. Matsushita is all ready to produce these things. Trust me, it's going to turn out to be a great investment."

"Trust you?" he spat. "Mr. Scherr, I would not trust you with...how do you Americans say?...my son's piggy bank. I am getting on a plane to New York where I will be charging you with embezzlement. And we have the attorneys and contacts in New York to do this and to make sure you pay the price for this."

A meeting was set at our attorney's offices in New York for the following week. The dour-faced president of the Dutch bank arrived accompanied by his equally somber-looking chief security officer. "What's he here for?" I whispered to Frank. "Is he worried I'm going to try and make a run for it?"

Frank didn't laugh.

The Mees and Hope people were accompanied by their counsel, a lawyer from a prestigious New York law firm who wore a pinstripe suit and wingtips.

It was obvious that they were out for blood...mine!

I was nervous but confident that I had made the transaction in good faith. Plus, our attorney—sitting next to me, studying some of our documents—was from a White Shoe firm, also. In fact, I noticed as I saw the threesome approaching, he even dressed like their lawyer. Still, I felt he was the right guy to be defending us.

I didn't realize how correct my assessment was. Divine providence must have been on our side that day, because when we entered the conference room, my attorney looked up, saw their attorney, and broke into laughter.

"Alistair, old man," said my lawyer. "I didn't know you were handling this."

"Nat!" said his attorney, excitedly. "I haven't seen you since the last reunion. Where've you been? How's Elaine?"

They were old Yale classmates. What followed was ten minutes of reminiscing about Harvard-Yale games of decades past, shenanigans in the residence halls, and old classmates. Before they got to the point where they were breaking out the family photos, my attorney earned his fee by telling his old buddy that, oh by the way, even though this Walter J. Scherr character may not have been Ivy League material, he was a decent enough chap trying to make an honest living, who would never do anything like trying to embezzle funds.

At that point, I stood up straight and tried to look honest and trustworthy.

The other attorney assessed me coldly. "Okay, Nate," he said. "So what are we going to do here?"

Not missing a beat, my attorney gave him the offer: We would use $150K to maintain the company and put the remaining $300K in escrow until the public offering in November. The $150K was for the lab and equipment so Frank, working with Matsushita, could come up with the prototypes needed. Additional incentive from Mees and Hope was that once we had the public offering we could keep the $300K, and the banker would add $600K to the public offering.

"Sounds reasonable," said Alistair. He looked at the president of Mees and Hope, who at this point was probably beginning to sense that I was not the devious criminal he had thought—and also realized that if he still wished to pursue a charge of fraud, he'd probably need a lawyer from another college. He took a deep breath, and nodded.

"All right," he said.

We were saved—or given a reprieve I should say.

Because while we had avoided debtor's prison, and now had the money we needed, we still needed a successful public offering to launch our enterprise properly.

Eventually, I found it—in large part by networking my way into a group of investors who socialized in a then-obscure part of Manhattan called SoHo.

I journeyed into this off-the-beaten part of the city because I heard that this was where some of the city's savvy investors and brokers congregated, and I wanted to ensure that all of these brokers were aware that we were going public. This way they would know me, the company, and how we were going to revolutionize the technology—

and, I hoped, they would want to buy some of the stock from our broker in November.

Back in the 1970s, the only people who lived in SoHo were artists. They appreciated the cheap rents, the huge industrial spaces, and the light that flowed through the floor-to-ceiling windows with their unobstructed views of lower Manhattan. SoHo was a totally new experience for me, as was the huge, open, sparely decorated loft where these brokers socialized, played high stakes card games, and if the mood struck them...made investments. Huge paintings, unlike anything I'd seen before, hung on plain white walls. The owner was a broker whose artist friends had turned him on to the neighborhood. The broker supported them by buying their art for not a lot of money (he later made a fortune selling some of the pieces at auctions).

Finding the place was always an adventure, because most cabbies had never heard of SoHo and didn't know how to navigate its narrow, cobblestone streets. The area was deserted after dark, no lights, no stores or restaurants. Getting into the building felt like something out of Prohibition days. I half expected that some tough mug would demand the secret password when I pushed the buzzer to enter the building.

The guests were mostly stockbrokers and clients from New York City and Westchester. All the brokers were in the process of issuing IPOs. I don't know if it's like this now in Silicon Valley, but this is the way it was in the nascent high-tech industry of the 1970s: You'd see guys from ten firms sitting around a table, and over drinks, each one would provide a brief sketch about his deal to the other guys, who would then buy stock and hold it in their company's name. There was a tacit agreement to hold onto the other guy's stock so as not to disrupt the market. It was in this unusual environment that Visual Sciences finally found its backers.

It had taken a lot of cold calls, a lot of meetings, and a few round-about cab drives through the mean streets of SoHo. But during one of these informal but powerful get-togethers, I found that the talk turned to Visual Sciences, and by the end of the evening we had generated interest for the public offering. The whole process was as smooth as the single malt scotches they were sipping that night, and tasted just as good.

When we finally issued our initial public offering in November of 1970—the only company to do so in the last half of that year, which had been marked by a crash in technology stocks in April—I felt as if we'd achieved a miracle.

According to the report filed by the Securities and Exchange Commission for 1970, Visual Sciences offered 200,000 shares at a price of $7 per share to "engage in the distribution of facsimile equipment for the transmission of graphic and documentary materials." Reading it today, I bet there was a lot of head scratching as to exactly what "facsimile" equipment was. But people were starting to catch on. And now, I thought, Xerox wasn't the only player in this market.

Matsushita had agreed to produce the units by the third or fourth quarter of 1971. Now we needed distributors for our new Visual Sciences business fax machines in Europe and the U.S. For the former, the Plessey Company was at the top of my list. I had gotten to know them when I lived in London, so as soon as I had a prototype, I approached them. Plessey didn't manufacture any products; they were a major telecommunications company that specialized in transporting data along already established networks. I knew their president, who was proud of his resemblance to the suave British film actor David Niven. I called him David and he loved it.

I set out to convince David that he and Plessy should take a chance on Visual Sciences, to be a pioneer in Europe with a new form of communication.

In the spring of 1971, one of our brokers hosted a party in Jacksonville, Florida, to promote our stock. I invited David, a well-known figure in the world of telecommunications, and the broker shrewdly arranged for the mayor of Jacksonville to honor him for his contributions to the industry. David eagerly accepted the invitation to receive his award (I'm sure the idea of escaping the dreary British weather for sunny Florida didn't hurt).

He was the big man on campus that day, and he reveled in all the attention. Also present at the reception was a beautiful young woman named Mary Lou. She had been born and bred in Alabama, and she spoke with a honey-thick southern drawl. I made the introductions.

"Y'all look just lahk that movie star Day-vud Niven," she said. "He's so haynd-sum."

I thought the glass of gin and tonic was going to shatter in David's hand. Within fifteen minutes of meeting her, he had decided he had to hire Mary Lou to be his executive secretary. Although she was very attractive, Mary Lou's looks weren't the main draw. David, it turned out, loved the idea of being the only managing director in England whose secretary had a gen-u-wyne American southern drawl.

"Say it again, please, Mary Lou," I heard him asking her at the reception. "I just love the way you say it."

"Say whut?" she'd tease. "You mean...Lun-dun, Ayngland?"

"Marvelous!" he'd exclaim. "No one, my dear, has ever pronounced the name of our capitol city that way."

David grabbed my arm and demanded to know whether I thought she'd be interested in moving to London to work for him. At first, I wasn't comfortable with this. What exactly did he have in mind? He quickly assured me that he would treat her with utmost respect and swore there'd be no "hanky-panky" on his part.

I hoped I could trust his assurances and agreed to discuss his request with our host, who had invited Mary Lou. She must have been ready to explore life abroad and new experiences, because she quickly accepted David's offer.

There was a glitch: According to British labor law, non-British citizens were prohibited from being hired for jobs that could be filled by citizens of the United Kingdom. The government saw no good reason to import an American when so many British citizens were eligible to be David's secretary. Nevertheless, David was determined to hire Mary Lou. Perhaps because I'd worked for British Sperry for three years, he was convinced that I could find a way to circumvent British immigration law. In fact, I had come up with an idea about how to make his dream come true. And if David owed us a favor, it could work to Visual Sciences' benefit.

I wrote the British authorities a long letter, explaining that Visual Sciences was about to launch a totally new method of communications. We had commenced negotiations with Plessey to be our British partner in this venture. Mary Lou had received extensive training and experience in this new field. Plessey therefore required her presence in order to ensure the success of our joint American-British program. The letters between the British authorities and me flew back and forth for many weeks, until they finally agreed to allow Plessey to hire Mary Lou. Both David and I were very pleased—for very different reasons. He was happy to have the only secretary in Lun-dun, probably in all of England, who greeted callers and visitors with a cheerful "How y'all doin' today?"

I was happy because now he owed me a rather large favor, which I would redeem as soon as possible.

A month later, I flew to England. My first appointment was with David. On the way to his executive suite, I checked in with Mary Lou who had her office outside his. As someone who felt partially responsible for all this, I was hoping she was not regretting her decision to uproot.

"Wahlt-uh!" she said when she saw me. "Ah heard you were visitin' today. So nahce to see yew."

She was a beauty, and with that drawl, I could see why they all were enamored with her. The feeling was mutual. She told me that she loved working for David, and she'd made many friends at Plessey. Before arriving in England, she'd never been north of the Mason-Dixon line, much less to another continent. Now, she'd already spent a weekend in France and was planning a trip to Ireland in the near future. Life in London was one great adventure after another. As for David, he was as proud and pleased as if he'd actually won an Oscar.

When I took him for drinks at my favorite pub, where I was delighted to see many of my old pals, David thanked me repeatedly for all my efforts on his behalf. Just as he'd hoped, Mary Lou's gracious southern demeanor had made him the envy of his peers in the communications industry. I bought him another ale and we toasted Mary Lou. Now it was time to return the favor. I good-naturedly reminded him of all the effort I'd expended so that Plessey could hire Mary Lou. When I suggested that Plessey should consider buying and distributing 150 machines to test the size of the British market, he slapped the table.

"Splendid idea, old boy," he said, then hailed the barman and pointed to our empty pint glasses. "Same again, for my new business partner and me."

The next day, slightly hung over, I flew to Japan to inform Matsushita that Plessey had agreed to be our European distributor. As Plessey was well respected in Japan, Matsushita was most pleased with my announcement. The American financial community also liked the Plessey connection, so our stock price began to rise.

One more task to resolve: finding a distributor in the United States. I had someone in mind: a fast-growing Minnesota-based company that had started in the early 1900s as a mining concern, and had later switched to producing adhesives. By the early 1970s, they were already a major corporation with diversified products that included audiotapes and photocopying technology.

Just a few years later, in 1980, they would become a household name thanks to the introduction of one of the most successful office products of all time: Post-it Notes. But even prior to that, the 3M Corporation—which stood for Minnesota Mining and Manufacturing—was already a company poised for great things.

I really wanted to hitch our wagon to them.

Plessey had just received the initial shipment of twenty fax machines from Japan and was in the process of placing them with their key customers. I suggested to the 3M people that we visit Plessey to see the machines in action. Like Mary Lou, the 3M executives I was dealing with had never been outside the United States, so they were naturally very eager to visit England. Unlike Mary Lou, however, their "Minne-soder" accents were about as warm and comforting as a blast of icy wind off Lake Superior.

No problem. As a favor to me, David met them and put on the Niven-esque charm. He was the perfect host for the 3M people. He introduced them to the customers, arranged for sightseeing trips, accompanied them to the most popular nightclubs, and even invited them to his home for dinner. Mary Lou came along a couple of times, and managed to charm the Minnesotans as surely as she'd charmed the Brits.

The trip to England was a great success. Thanks to David, the 3M group saw firsthand the multiple uses of Visual Sciences' fax machines.

My time-consuming correspondence with the British government regarding Mary Lou's employment had certainly paid off, and then some.

Next stop was Japan again, so the 3M execs could see for themselves how the machines and their components were manufactured. I managed to get them an invitation to the geisha house where I had met "Baby." They had such a good time there that they all but begged me to take them back again. I would have done just about anything short of murder to secure a distribution contract with them, so I persuaded our Japanese hosts to arrange a second visit. They were impressed by Matsushita's factory assembly line, but they were even more excited by their two visits to the geisha house. The combination of the two experiences added up to an order for 150 machines.

We now had international and domestic distribution contracts, and the market recognized that we were going to be a formidable force that could compete against Xerox.

What I needed now was a veteran salesman with experience in this area; someone who could also teach the people at 3M how to sell a technology many had never even heard of. I knew just the man.

I took a trip to Chicago to look up my old friend from Litton Industries, Jim McCarthy. I was sure that Jim, who was then working in sales and marketing at a major corporation, would be the ideal mentor for the 3M sales reps, just as he had been my mentor in Europe.

I took him to dinner in the Loop, looked him in the eyes, and asked:

"Jim, my dear friend, tell me something. Do you love me?"

He rolled his eyes. "Yes, Walter, you know I do. Just don't tell me again about Grandma McCue. I've heard that story six times."

I laughed. "What can I say, Jim? I love my family and I love my friends..." I picked up my glass and toasted him. "And because you're like family to me, I've got something to ask you. Do you think you could you sell one hundred and fifty fax machines in two to three months?"

"Tall order," he said, rubbing his chin with his hand. "But I know that whatever you and Frank make is going to be a quality product. So... sure. I think I could sell at least a hundred."

"Great! Okay, so now I have a proposition for you."

Jim fluttered his eyelids and looked up dramatically, feigning the embarrassed coquette. "Walter, I know you love me...but remember, I'm married."

"Very funny. Seriously now. If you come to work for Visual Sciences, I will give you stock options that could make you financially independent for the rest of your life."

He sat upright, looking slightly stunned. But then he smiled warily. "Assuming, that is, that the company is successful. Otherwise that stock won't be worth a damn."

I nodded. "That's right. But with you and me and Frank working together...and with 3M and Plessey involved...I don't think that's going to be the case. I think we can make great things happen here."

Jim stuck out his hand. "I agree. Count me in."

I ignored his outstretched paw and hugged him instead.

The next day, I called a meeting at a hotel in Minneapolis, where I introduced Jim to the salespeople. I told them that with his thirty years of telecommunication sales experience, Jim would spend a week teaching them about the industry in general and about facsimile machines in particular. He would also come up with a list of prospects for each territory. The rule was that Jim would accompany each salesperson whenever they met with a customer. However, I added, while he was there to help, they—the 3M salesmen—would get credit (and commission) for each sale. This was my plan on how to utilize the great resource that was Jim McCarthy and still incentivize the salesforce.

It worked: Within three months, they sold all 150 machines. The four salesmen were ecstatic, and if Jim wasn't married I might have proposed to him right there!

3M owned a beautiful retreat with cabins and a lodge on a lake in northern Minnesota. I now wanted to thank the salesmen by hosting a reception there. I told 3M that I would pay for all the expenses—dinner, drinks, and the use of the cabins—and invited all their top marketing and sales executives. I was the master of ceremonies, but I introduced each of the four salesmen individually on stage, because I wanted them to know how much we appreciated and valued their efforts.

I left there feeling very pleased by the results of the reception—and about where our new venture was headed. 3M had given Visual Sciences a one-year order for three thousand machines.

Look out Xerox: We had established ourselves as major players!

By the mid-1970s, Wall Street and the industry knew Visual Sciences. No longer were people asking us "what's a fax machine?" They were becoming more accepted as a communications tool.

I felt that I was now about to take my place as a major player in what they said would be a billion-dollar industry.

As it turned out, they were right, but I was wrong.

The Story Inside the Story:
WALTER'S WAY

WHY I WROTE THIS BOOK:

*How
Heart Surgery
Launched Me
Onto My Greatest
Discovery*

Graduates of the Discovery Scholarship Program thank Walter for his support

MY DISCOVERY
Walter Scherr

When I was a young man of eighty and working at Veeco (an experience you can read about in Chapter 10 of this book), I was diagnosed with an almost total blockage of my carotid artery. My doctor told me that unless I immediately had surgery, I could suffer a stroke or even die. When I mentioned my dire situation to a colleague, Jack Rein, he told me that his brother-in-law, Dr. George Todd, was the number one carotid artery surgeon in the country. Jack immediately called and arranged for me to see Dr. Todd that same day. He performed the surgery at Mount Sinai/St. Luke's Roosevelt Medical Center in New York, and I was soon able to return to work. When I went to see Dr. Todd later for a checkup, I thanked him again for saving my life.

"Would you like to show your gratitude by making a donation to the hospital?" he asked.

"No, thanks," I said.

St. Luke's Roosevelt (now merged with Mt. Sinai) is an excellent hospital. But the reason I deferred was that several

Veeco employees were parents of children who had cerebral palsy. My family had recently established a foundation to support these children and their families. Dr. Todd was clearly surprised by my answer. "What causes do you support?" he asked.

When I started to talk about the foundation, Dr. Todd began to smile. "I think I can help you out with that," he said. He told me that he had a son who was a resident at The Center for Discovery, an organization that provided care and treatment for people with significant disabilities. As a father and a doctor, he was very impressed with the Center. He would welcome the perspective of a businessman. Would I accompany him to visit there and give him some feedback?

He'd aroused my curiosity, and I could hardly say no again, so I went up to The Center, which is located in New York's Sullivan County. I toured the facilities, talked to residents and caregivers, and observed the professional staff. I found a community suffused with the spirit of Mother Teresa (who I had met in India in 1967); a community that practiced compassion, promoted innovation, ignored barriers, and embraced possibilities.

When I returned home, I sent a letter to Patrick Dollard, The Center's President and CEO, , and Richard Humleker, the Vice President of Development, along with a check for $100,000. I expressed "my thanks and admiration to you and your associates for helping God's children live more independent lives. The trip reminded me that there are many people whose career choices inherently add value to our society, and whose life work advances the greater good."

This was the beginning of a journey that is now more than ten years old. We have accomplished many of our goals, but we still have much more work to accomplish. I wrote this book to raise awareness of The Center's outstanding work on behalf of children and adults with disabilities. Our long-range goal is to disseminate The Center's evidence-based practices on a worldwide basis. You can read more about The Center in the following pages. That's why one hundred percent of the proceeds from the sale of this book are going to support their mission.

Walter Scher

Pre-Depression days at the sea.

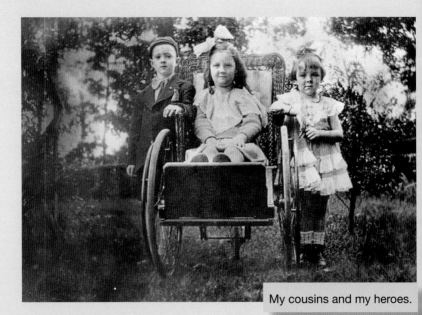

My cousins and my heroes.

Our wedding day, 1953: The beginning of a marriage that lasted 50 years and produced four children, 11 grandchildren and two great grandchildren. (Vera passed in 2003).

Sunday Mass, 1966.

NOVEMBER 6, 1974

BOTH OF VISUAL SCIENCES, INC AND MATSUSHITA GRAPHIC COMMUNICATION SYSTEMS. INC HAVE NOW COME TO CELEBRATE THE 5TH ANNIVERSARY OF THE MUTUAL RELATIONSHIP.

THE BUSINESS COOPERATION BETWEEN THE COMPANIES HAS BEEN ENHANCED TO HAVE A CLOSEST TIE-UP WHICH HAS SUBSTANTIALLY CONTRIBUTED TO THE PROGRESS OF WORLD'S FACSIMILE INDUSTRY.

IT IS OWING TO YOU, MR. WALTER SCHERR, VERY MUCH THAT WE HAVE HAD A FIRM BELIEF WE SHOULD CONTRIBUTE TOWARD THE WORLD'S PEACE THROUGH THE CLOSER, MORE INTIMATE AND PERPETUAL RELATIONSHIP BETWEEN BOTH OF OUR COMPANIES.

IT IS MY GREAT HONOR AND HAPPINESS, REPRESENTING ALL MEMBERS OF THE BOARD AND EMPLOYEES OF MATSUSHITA GRAPHIC COMMUNICATION SYSTEMS, INC, TO SINCERELY APPRECIATE WHAT YOU HAVE ACHIEVED IN OUR RELATIONSHIP AND TO HEREBY PRESENT THE POSITION " HONORARY FRIEND OF THE COMPANY ".

CHIKAYUKI KINO
PRESIDENT

Honorary Friend of Japan, 1974.

First public facsimile company, November 1970.

The year is 1970 and the question I was being asked was, "What is a fax machine?"

Japan, 1966 (I am on the right): We were treated like rock stars.

Honoring caregivers.

My Inspiration, Mother Teresa, whom I met in India.

First well, 1985: Valence Operating Company.

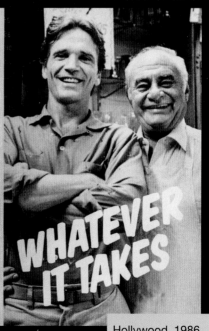

A FILM BY BOB DEMCHUK

WHATEVER IT TAKES

Starring
TOM MASON
CHRIS WEATHERHEAD
JAMES REBHORN
MAURA SHEA
and
MARTIN BALSAM as "HAP"

Screenplay
CHRIS WEATHERHEAD and BOB DEMCHUK

Music Score
GARRY SHERMAN

Songs
PETER UDELL and GARRY SHERMAN

Editor
BOB DEMCHUK

Director of Photography
JOHN DRAKE

Executive Producer
WALTER J. SCHERR

Producer/Director
BOB DEMCHUK

Hollywood, 1986.

Veeco

Proudly Honors

WALTER J. SCHERR

For His Many Years of
Dedication, Guidance and Integrity
Contributing to the Growth and
Success of Veeco Instruments Inc.

July 2006

To all Veeco employees:
The lives we live and the things we do sometimes get in the way of what we wish to say. Today I give thanks to those who have touched my heart in many ways. May God bless you and grant you health wisdom and peace.

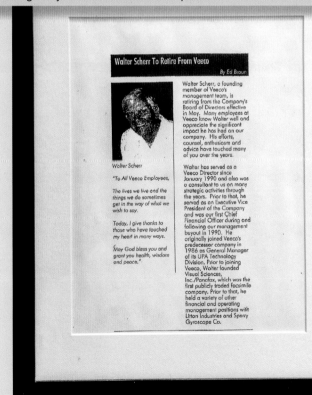

Walter Scherr To Retire From Veeco

By Ed Braun

Walter Scherr

"To All Veeco Employees,

The lives we live and the things we do sometimes get in the way of what we wish to say.

Today, I give thanks to those who have touched my heart in many ways.

May God bless you and grant you health, wisdom and peace."

Walter Scherr, a founding member of Veeco's management team, is retiring from the Company's Board of Directors effective in May. Many employees at Veeco know Walter well and appreciate the significant impact he has had on our company. His efforts, counsel, enthusiasm and advice have touched many of you over the years.

Walter has served as a Veeco Director since January 1990 and also was a consultant to us on many strategic activities through the years. Prior to that, he served as an Executive Vice President of the Company and was our first Chief Financial Officer during and following our management buyout in 1990. He originally joined Veeco's predecessor company in 1986 as General Manager of its UPA Technology Division. Prior to joining Veeco, Walter founded Visual Sciences, Inc./Panafax, which was the first publicly traded facsimile company. Prior to that, he held a variety of other financial and operating management positions with Litton Industries and Sperry Gyroscope Co.

A view into The Center's bio-dynamically certified Thanksgiving Farm CSA (Community Supported Agriculture) that opened in 1993. It features four 5-bed residences (Parsley, Sage, Rosemary and Thyme) and is critical to providing an annual bounty of great food to The Center's Department of Nourishment Arts, as well as to its residents and hundreds of CSA members.

Led by members of The Center's Outdoor Education Team, two non-ambulatory Center residents head off up the trail in specially-designed action track wheelchairs to discover and explore places they've never been able to get to before!

Kyle enjoys getting out of his wheelchair for a better view! Just having fun!

A little independence...

(L-R: Bud Scherr, Walter J. Scherr, Douglas Scherr, Laura Saggese.)

Walter J. Scherr and his family at 'Walter's Way,'
a street on The Center for Discovery campus, named in
recognition of his generous support. You can help, too!

Visit www.waltersway.org

7

INTERNATIONAL INTRIGUES

I STOOD ON THE 59TH FLOOR OF CHASE MANHATTAN'S HEADQUARTERS, gazing out over the city's downtown, which stretched out to a seemingly unlimited horizon. There was the spire of old Trinity Church, where George Washington prayed after taking the oath of office as first president of the new United States. There was the Woolworth Building on Broadway—once the tallest in the world; and near it, the building that now held that title, the new World Trade Center, its twin towers rising high. In the distance, the spans of the Verrazano Bridge, a colossus across the Narrows to Staten Island, dominated the skyline. And in the harbor, the Statue of Liberty raised her lamp gracefully into the clear late morning air.

It was a magnificent view, and yet almost as breathtaking to me was the viewpoint.

As we admired the city sprawled out beneath us, I couldn't help but turn to sneak a glance at the man standing next to me. It was in his offices we now stood. Could this really be? Could the guy from Ozone Park—the Relief Kid who survived the Depression; the 28-year-old soda jerk; the naive young manager who almost had his career terminated because he bungled the company's parking policy—really be standing shoulder-to-shoulder with the scion of the most powerful family in American history; a family whose name was synonymous with wealth?

David Rockefeller, Jr. caught my eye, and smiled. "Nice view, isn't it, Walter?" he said. "I never get tired of it."

I stammered out an agreement. Despite the ease and cordiality with which he had greeted me when I arrived minutes earlier, I still wasn't sure whether I should be calling him David, Mr. Rockefeller, or Your Eminence. One reason the streets bustled beneath us was because of his decision to construct the bank's gleaming 60-story headquarters in downtown Manhattan. The building, One Chase Plaza, was completed in 1961. Rockefeller, then president of Chase, had been instrumental in the bank's decision to locate to the Wall Street area. Its construction had helped to revive the Financial District.

David, Jr. was the grandson of John D. Rockefeller, the founder of Standard Oil and the man who built the family's fortune, once the largest in the world. As I got to know David Rockefeller that morning and in subsequent interactions, I realized that although he'd been born into almost unimaginable wealth, he hadn't bought his way into the president's office. There were plenty of other sons and grandsons of tycoons who weren't running one of the most important financial institutions in the world. David earned his position: he was smart and gracious, and from the first time we met, he made me feel we were meeting on an equal playing field.

The meeting that day in the spring of 1977 had been brokered by Jim McLinden, Vice President of Technology at Chase Manhattan

Bank and an old friend from Sperry. Jim and I would catch up over lunch periodically. At one of our lunches, Jim told me that his boss wanted to meet me; I almost jumped out of my chair.

Now, here I was, at these dizzying heights. Rockefeller probably knew the effect his surname had on people, and I think he sought to bring both of my feet back to the ground as quickly as possible. He had greeted me with a warm smile. "Jim's told me you're a great customer," he said, extending his hand. "I'm happy to meet someone in a growing industry, and I'd like to do whatever I can to help."

We'd come from very different places: While I had been banking the furnace, he was being groomed to own the bank. Still, as we sat chatting over lunch in his private dining room with the breathtaking view, I found that he and I had some things in common. We were both interested in finance and politics. David had his opinions and so did I. But what we really shared was our belief that nothing was more important in life than having a close circle of family and friends. David was as proud of his six children as I was of my four, and I soon found myself swapping photos and stories about the respective successes of our kids in the classroom, the football field, the basketball court. I forgot that I was with a man who was worth (in today's terms) about three billion dollars.

For that hour or so, he was just another dad, like me.

We met several more times for lunch, and it was then that David asked for my help. He'd tried repeatedly to contact financial officers at Matsushita, but they had shown no interest in talking to him. I knew that Japanese companies dealt only with Japanese banks. Nevertheless, I was surprised that the Rockefeller name had not been enough to entice them to discuss even the possibility of doing business with Chase. David happily accepted my offer to convey an invitation from him to the appropriate people at Matsushita.

I'd like to think it was the Scherr name that turned the tables. More likely somebody in Tokyo finally noticed the surname of the man I was trying to make introductions for. A reply came: "Of course, we will meet with Mr. Rockefeller."

Whatever my role, David was very grateful for our help in setting up this meeting. And truth be told, he had come to the right man: Over the previous few years, we had developed such a close relationship with Matsushita that I felt like what the kids today would say, their BFF; or to use the Japanese phrase: *shinyu*—best friend.

I even have the document to prove it.

Visual Sciences had recruited a world-class technical team, and we had become competitive in the market. We had invested three million dollars to update the Matsushita plant in Tokyo. They had produced top quality machines, including fax machines with a stack feeder that accepted all kinds of paper of varying weights. The market for fax machines had become a billion dollar industry, growing at a rate of 30 to 40 percent a year.

We had helped Matsushita make enormous profits in this new industry. They knew it, and they seemed to appreciate it. Just a few years before my lunch with David Rockefeller, in November of 1974, the company had held a dinner in Japan to commemorate the fifth anniversary of our partnership. I was presented with a plaque, written in delicate Japanese calligraphy, which praised our joint business venture and pledged a "closer...perpetual relationship" between our two companies. I was also named an "Honorary Friend of the Company" and praised to the skies.

"It is very much owing to you, Mr. Walter Scherr," read the inscription, "that we firmly believe we should contribute toward world's peace through the closer, more intimate and perpetual relationship of both our companies."

At some point that evening, one of the executives at Matsushita that we'd worked closely with suggested it was time for us to become real partners and go into business together in the United States. He knew, as did Konosuke Matsushita, the founder and namesake of the company, that Visual Sciences' contract with 3M included a clause that permitted us to distribute our products in the United States at the end of the initial five-year period of our agreement. Although Visual Sciences was a profitable company, we couldn't afford to create our own distribution network in the U.S. without a huge injection of additional funds. But if Matsushita were willing to finance us, we could then take responsibility for the day-to-day operations.

I was urged to create a planning document that would outline in detail the risks and rewards of entering the American market. I had to cover every aspect of what we needed in order to successfully lease and/or sell our machines. I was excited by this opportunity and worked on the joint venture document every spare moment I had for an entire year. The finished product was virtually a how-to on running a business in the emerging American fax industry. It covered everything from service strategy and manufacturing costs to a competitive analysis of all the other players in the market.

When I was finally done, I reviewed the business plan with some of the top executives at Matsushita, including the namesake himself— a man who had just a few years earlier appeared on the cover of *Time* magazine as the face of Asia's rising prosperity. He thought I'd done a very good job. Then Matsushita management threw a curve ball at me. It was important to respect the Japanese culture of consensus, they said. "Of course!" I replied, nodding, not really certain what that meant. I quickly learned that building consensus would require me to spend the next two months at their headquarters in Osaka, standing on a stage in an auditorium, reviewing every aspect of the plan for a room full of Matsushita employees. Without this step, I was assured, they wouldn't be able to sell the plan to their people. Here was a striking difference in the business cultures of our two countries. I had to stifle a laugh at the very thought of what some of the hard-edged chief executives at Sperry would have said had they been urged to build "employee consensus" for a new business initiative. To that generation of American managers, running a corporation was like commanding an army. You gave the orders, the soldiers followed them.

Not here. I was on stage with an interpreter for ten hours a day, six days a week, reviewing the details, the risks, and the rewards of entering the biggest market in the world in front of an audience of employees of all levels. It was an exhausting ordeal, going over the same material again and again, repeatedly answering the same questions. But when all of the queries had been asked and answered, and we finally had a deal, I went home feeling I'd met my goal.

We agreed that because Matsushita was going to fund the project, they would have 51 percent ownership of the joint venture, and Visual Sciences had the remaining 49 percent. Frank and I hadn't been totally pleased with that split, but we had known we couldn't raise the hundreds of millions of dollars we would need for distribution, service organization, diagnostic centers—everything that we'd require to compete on our own with companies like Xerox, which already dominated the market. Mr. Matsushita had assured me that no decisions would be made without our input and agreement. We were entering into a "closer, more intimate and perpetual relationship of both our companies."

It said so on the plaque.

Despite the unequal split, I was proud to be in business with this company; I was proud to be known as an "Honorary Friend." Sad to say, it would turn out that their view of friendship was very different from mine.

***

There was a wide world out there that was waking up to the potential of the fax machine. In the early 1970s, we were Matsushita's exclusive worldwide distributor for fax machines, with sales, service, and support in forty countries. In order to position Visual Sciences as an international company that could meet those needs, we bought a flat in London, which served as our business office and also provided first-class accommodations for our business guests.

It was also the jumping-off point for me to visit potential clients and distributors in Europe. Very often these trips ended with a deal. But one of them produced one of the single most terrifying experiences of my life.

I had gone to visit a major equipment operator in the German city of Dusseldorf. I wanted them to become a partner of Visual Sciences. The head of the firm was impressed with our company, and wanted to work with us, but he told me I'd need to talk to their division head in the Netherlands.

Fine, I thought. I'll drive to the Netherlands and close this deal face-to-face. I hopped in my rental car, and drove west. Or at least that's where I thought I was driving. This was of course long before the advent of GPS technology in automobiles, and the road maps I had were in German, as were the road signs. Soon, I got lost. Very lost.

Dusseldorf is on the Rhine River in the western part of the country then known as West Germany. I ended up driving almost straight East.

Today, it would have likely meant a pleasant, if unintended diversion. In those years, it meant that I was driving straight towards the Communist nation of East Germany, an enemy of the West.

As I drove on, I noticed that the countryside was growing sparser, more barren. It was getting dark and I was getting frustrated. I picked up speed, hoping to see someplace where I might find someone who spoke English and could point me in the right direction.

I rounded a curve and suddenly found myself driving straight into a cluster of barriers, with signs in German in large capital letters.

I had inadvertently driven right into the East German border.

Lights flashed, I heard commotion and shouts. A group of armed, uniformed men rushed out of nowhere to surround my car. They shouted at me in German, and pointed their guns at my head.

"American!" I shouted, raising my hands. "American!"

No one lowered their weapons, but one of them inched forward and motioned at me to get out of the car and come forward.

"Hände nach oben!" he shouted. "Hands up."

I didn't speak German, but I instinctively threw my hands over my head. In my right hand, was my passport, which I'd had enough sense to grab before I got out. A group of these border patrolmen swarmed around my car as I was led past the gates and into what looked like an old railroad shack a few hundred yards across the border. My passport was ripped out of my hand along the way. Nobody said "Welcome to the German Democratic Republic," the official name of what we called East Germany. They didn't need to. By then, even hopelessly lost Walter had realized where he was.

The lead guard, whose face I could barely make out with the flashlights in my face, had figured out that I didn't speak German. He gestured again, this time with the muzzle of gun, into the interior of the shack. I walked in, and heard them slam and bolt the door behind me.

For the next four hours, I sat alone in that room, praying, wishing, hoping, pleading. I've always prided myself on being a good Catholic, but that afternoon I promised God that I'd become one of the All-Time Great Catholics—if he'd only help me get out of this fix. My situation was grim. No one from our London office knew where I was. I couldn't communicate with my captors. Even if I could, I doubt they would understand what a "facsimile" machine was—or care.

At one point, I even worried about my own German surname. Would that raise suspicions, I worried?

During the interminable time in that shack, I remember hearing a creaking outside the door, and I thought I saw someone peek through the cracks. I felt cold eyes assessing me.

In retrospect, I can laugh about this, as I imagine what they observed: A skinny, scared, middle-aged guy from Queens with glasses. I don't know what the German translation is for "Comrade, no way could this nerd be a Western intelligence agent!" but I suspect something akin to that assessment was offered in the discussion that ensued among the guards, or between officials at this particular border crossing and East Berlin or wherever they reported to. Because after what seemed like the entire evening, the door opened, my not-so-friendly guard appeared again, handed me my passport and escorted me back to my car, which someone had turned around, so that it was now facing the opposite direction.

"Verlassen!" he barked. "Leave."

I was only too happy to oblige. But when I tried at first, I realized that my hands were shaking so badly I couldn't even put the key in the ignition. Finally, with an act of will and a deep breath, I steadied myself, started the car, and verlassened as fast as I could.

***

After years of planning and working, the day came when we were finally able to celebrate our joint venture with Matsushita. Our dream of being ground-breaking pioneers in the field of telecommunications was becoming a reality. We had built a world-class headquarters for our newly created Panafax enterprise in Woodbury, New York. Mr. Matsushita and his five top executives flew over from Japan for the opening ceremony. He couldn't stop grinning when I introduced him to our expert technical team. He knew them by reputation, and he greeted all of them warmly.

We gave Mr. Matsushita the honor of cutting the ribbon to officially initiate our joint venture. As I stood next to him and smiled for the cameras, I was still concerned about that 51/49 stock split. Whenever I brought up the subject, I was assured that it was only on paper. For all practical purposes, he would honor our relationship as if we were equal partners. I took these men at their word. We had known each other for ten years, from the time I had helped extricate his company from that sticky situation with Litton. Our families had met; we had visited each other's homes, spent time together at weddings and other special occasions.

Besides, I knew that honor and face meant a great deal in Japanese culture. We were business associates, but we were also friends.

We named our new joint venture Panafax, and I became Executive Vice President for Operations. We spent the next three years building the leading facsimile company in the United States. I became known as someone who understood Japanese business and knew how to build mutually profitable relationships. No less a personage than David Rockefeller had sought me ought for this reason. All I needed was a few more Japanese language lessons, and I probably could have set myself up in a comfortably rewarding consultant position, advising companies on how to do business with the Japanese.

After all, I was an "Honorary Friend."

Right. I might as well have been wearing a dunce cap in international business. I just didn't realize it was sitting there on my head.

Some of the particulars are still puzzling to me, almost 40 years later. The way I saw it at the time, Matsushita tried to sabotage and destroy our company. To be fair, they may have seen it very differently, perhaps believing that the relationship wasn't as advantageous to them as they had originally thought.

A more objective source, *Fortune* magazine, writing about it in the 1980s, described Matsushita's attempt to bypass my colleagues and me in order to deal directly with important customers as "clumsy."

Here's what happened:

During the fourth year of our partnership, just as business was on a serious upswing, I started to notice small changes taking place in our relationship. The first was the unexpected arrival of people from headquarters, who had been sent over, they would tell me in heavily-accented English, to be the new sales or service representative or the new financial accountant. I'd tell headquarters that I hadn't asked for these people; and I already had competent people in those positions—people who could speak English fluently, which was a requirement if you were going to do business in the United States.

Matsushita would inevitably prevail, and suddenly I had five more employees on the payroll—employees who would stay late every night to fax information to Japan. I was so busy running the business that although I wondered what was going on, I didn't stop to ponder the implications. Even if I had, I'm not sure what I would have done if I'd realized what was happening. After all, they owned 51 percent of the company and we owned 49.

130

Then, suddenly, the phone calls from Japan stopped. I was used to being in regular contact with Matsushita executives in Osaka—men I knew well. But weeks went by without a word. My calls to them went unanswered.

Instead, I started getting disturbing calls from Plessey and other companies around the world, to tell me that National, the name Matsushita used to distribute its products in Europe, was selling the same machines as Plessey.

When Matsushita stopped delivering fax machines to us I realized we were in trouble.

In a last-ditch effort to find out what was going on, we decided to go to Japan and get some answers. I wasn't alone in my concerns. Visual Sciences' Board of Directors—who stood solidly behind me in this fight—was as puzzled as I was, and they wanted some answers too.

We were used to being greeted at the airport by Matsushita officials when we visited. It was a simple courtesy. This time, no one was there to meet us. That set the tone for the trip. We returned to New York with our questions unanswered, but resolved to fight. When we arrived, we drove straight to our attorneys' office and filed a motion for breach of contract, seeking to be awarded hundreds of millions of dollars.

In the ensuing legal action, Matsushita continued to treat us the way they had during our personal visit. They ignored us. Not one of their executives ever appeared in a courtroom to explain or defend their position. In desperation, I contacted New York State Senator Al D'Amato, who, like me, resided on Long Island; and U.S. ambassador to Japan, former Arkansas Senator Mike Mansfield. The politicians were sympathetic, and they tried to help us, but to no avail. Meanwhile, the judge tried to get both sides to compromise, also with little effect. The Japanese knew they held the cards. They knew that the mighty Matsushita corporation could easily outlast a few guys who were rapidly running out of money.

Still, we felt that we were in the right, and were willing to do whatever it took to resolve this. At age 55, I was willing to drain my personal retirement fund to help pay our legal fees. It wasn't nearly enough. Without sales and cash flow we were delisted from the stock exchange. Subsequent legal action against us from stockholders seemed to be the final blow in this David vs. Goliath showdown.

Desperate times call for desperate measures. Calling in a few favors, one of our board members managed to get us in touch with a lawyer whose very name usually struck fear in the hearts of his opponents: To say that Roy Cohn's reputation was checkered is an understatement. Cohn served in the early 1950s as chief counsel to Senator Joe McCarthy, the chairman of the Senate Permanent Subcommittee on Investigations. One of McCarthy's self-appointed missions was to purge alleged Communists from government agencies. His targets included the Voice of America, which broadcasted American news and culture to countries outside the United States. Ed Kretzman, a VOA policy advisor, characterized Roy Cohen as Senator McCarthy's "chief hatchet man."

By the time I met him, Federal investigators had charged him with professional misconduct. After a lengthy legal battle, the New York State Supreme Court disbarred him in 1986, just weeks before he died. Regardless of his rogue reputation, Mr. Cohn was known to be effective. His obituary in the *New York Times* described him as "flamboyant and controversial," but also "a ferociously loyal advocate." He was certainly an advocate for us. He provided us with valuable information that we used to make our bargaining position marginally stronger. Matsushita finally responded. We settled for a fraction of the true cost of the company, and I took a huge financial hit from the Panafax debacle. However, I can safely say that without Roy Cohn I would have had to declare bankruptcy.

I can also say that Matsushita today continues to be one of the world's great companies, and is no doubt managed now by a new generation of executives who would probably never have entered into the kind of agreement that caused us both such problems. Most Americans know Matsushita by the brand name it uses for its array of consumer electronics products: Panasonic.

Regardless of the fiasco, I would live to fight another day, in another industry. Just as the facsimile machine was reaching its potential, just as it was poised to realize its forecasted potential of a billion dollars, I was on the sidelines.

It was time to start a new game. This one would take me far from the executive suites and courtrooms of Manhattan; far from Tokyo and East Germany; far from the grim realities and harsh tactics of business and politics. I was headed for a place in which such things seemed irrelevant; a destination even more unlikely for the Relief Kid from Ozone Park than David Rockefeller's dining suite overlooking Manhattan.

Walter J. Scherr was bound for Hollywood.

The High Seas, Hollywood, and the Poker Boys

I'D SPENT THE LAST TWO YEARS FIGHTING A BRUISING LEGAL BATTLE WITH Matsushita. But we'd finally reached a favorable financial settlement, and I was no longer preoccupied by the fallout from our failed joint venture. I was ready to move forward, to find a business opportunity that would spark my curiosity and carry me into the future.

I found it through a network of friends from my past.

Back at Sperry, a group of us had formed a stock club in the 1950s. In the days before Internet day trading, this was a way you could play the market, have fun, and if you were smart, make a couple of bucks. Our Sperry stock club produced many more positive results than our initial goal to profit from well-informed investments. Perhaps just as important, we forged loyal and lasting friendships which endured even if ten or twenty years went by without seeing one another.

Over the years, some had advanced to the top of the executive ladder, either at Sperry, other equally prestigious companies, or prominent financial institutions and investment companies. Others, myself included, happened upon serendipitous career opportunities that reunited us with Sperry friends from our earliest days at the company.

Three of the stock club fellows left Sperry and the club to form a financial services group. One of their divisions gave seed money to promising new business ventures. Tony, a former vice president and general manager at a Chicago-based conglomerate, was one of their success stories. He'd used their seed money to lead a successful management buyout of his division. Now he needed more money to grow his company, Video Library Systems.

The ex-stock club guys pre-dated by thirty years the Emmy-nominated television show, *Shark Tank*. They matched promising entrepreneurs with potential investors. Some of us could afford to invest in companies if we liked the sound of them—and the person who was making the presentation. I was no Mark Cuban, but my friends told me that Tony was smart and ambitious. I admired the fact that he'd put all his savings into the buyout. He had to believe that the outcome was worth the risk. I'd never heard of Video Library Systems, a small company with headquarters on Long Island, but I liked his ideas and style. My investment translated into a 20% share in the company.

Video Library's concept was simple. The union that represented tanker fleet crews required that their members be provided with a specific number of entertainment hours per month—and the crews preferred movies over any other form of entertainment. Tanker fleets contracted with Video Library to buy movies, which were shipped to Mexico, Hong Kong, Greece, Germany ... whichever international port the tankers embarked from. The company owned two 40,000-square-foot factories; one on Long Island, and the other in Piraeus, Greece's largest harbor, and one of Europe's busiest ports. The movie reels were sent to Long Island or

Piraeus to be converted into VHS-formatted videos. These were shipped to Video Library's agents, who delivered 30 or 40 movies to the tanker, depending on the duration of its trip. At the same time, the agents retrieved the videos they'd dropped off the previous month.

Video Library, one of only two companies that supplied the movies, sold to almost 650 tankers. Its rival was a division of an English conglomerate, and it served close to 950 tankers. The competition between the companies was fierce, each of them vying to lure unaffiliated tankers. Tony's dream, and very likely that of his English counterpart, was to buy out the other company, monopolize the market, and increase Video Library's pricing power.

I was still in the grip of the Matsushita debacle , looking to recoup losses. We had agreed to liquidate Panafax. I was preoccupied with concluding our negotiations, and Video Library Systems was an interesting but minor blip on my screen. I was about to go into a meeting one day when I received an urgent message: Tony had suffered a major heart attack. I was next in line after Tony as majority stockholder, and the Board of Directors, to which I'd been elected, wanted me to temporarily take over Tony's responsibilities. The company would fall apart without someone in charge. I then left Visual Sciences and assumed the duties of acting president of the company to make sure we had continuity of management.

Sperry, Litton, Visual Sciences ... I'd inhabited a world of Defense Department contracts, radar and landing systems, navigational instruments and fax machines. I'd discovered a completely other universe, an industry I might never have known. If I'd continued on the same familiar career path, I might not have discovered the intersection between movies and tanker fleets.

Tony had put all his money into the company. He was in his early fifties, happily married, the proud father of three girls. Video Library Systems was his family's only source of income. His doctors couldn't predict when he'd be well enough to leave the hospital or how long he would need to recover. Two months later, Tony's secretary, who normally made a point of knocking even when the door was wide open, walked into my office, sank into the chair across from mine, and started to cry. She told me that she had received a call from Tony's wife. Tony had passed away in the hospital.

I was worried about Tony's wife: how she was coping, whether she had enough money, how she felt about my new title. I sent her a note to say I hoped we could talk sometime soon. Could I visit her, whenever it was convenient? She wrote back that she would rather drop by when I wasn't busy. She wanted to pick up some of Tony's things, and she needed to see his office one last time.

She seemed surprised that I'd kept my old office instead of moving into Tony's. We chatted for a few minutes. Then, she told me what I already knew, that all her assets were tied up in the company, and her only income was Tony's salary.

I'd had to withdraw most of the money in my retirement fund in order to pay the lawyers who'd represented me against Matsushita. But even after I redeposited the amount I'd withdrawn, I had enough left over from the Matsushita settlement to buy Tony's share of the company. I'd discussed this possibility with Vera, and she thought it was the right thing to do.

"I want to buy Tony's company, if you're willing to sell it to me," I said to his widow. "Talk to people you trust. I promise I'll give you a good price, but you should find out what they think, too."

"Why are you doing this?" she asked.

It was a fair question. She needed the money, but I sensed she didn't want my pity.

"I invested in Video Library Systems because I liked Tony, and I have a lot of respect for what he accomplished. I'll do whatever we can to keep it growing. Losing Tony was a tragedy for all of us. Most of all for you and your daughters, of course. You need to mourn for him without worrying about finances or what's happening to the company."

She almost smiled. "Thank you. I appreciate that. I'll get back to you as soon as I can. In the meantime, I'll go spend some time in his office. I need to pack up his books and pictures." She looked as if she were about to cry, but then she stopped herself. "You probably want to move your things over there."

I stood up to see her out. "I like this office. I'm in no rush to leave here," I said. I put my hand out to shake hers, and then I changed my mind and gave her a hug.

I wanted to tell her that eventually she would get over feeling so wounded and vulnerable. I stopped myself, because I had no right to assume I knew what she was feeling today or in a year from today. What I could do was pay her what the company was worth and keep my promise to expand the Video Library. I'd already figured out how to do that.

Every company I'd worked for had required that I perform due diligence. Before I'd invested in Video Library, I discovered that I had some very talented people on staff, quite a few of whom had worked on documentary films.

I had a hunch that creating our own, in-house documentaries could contribute to Video Library's growth and success. At the very least, they could help us increase revenue and attract new clients. With our own movie crew, writers, and camera crew, we could write and produce tanker safety films.

I bid and won a contract for 3 million dollars to produce a series of documentaries about ship safety in nine languages, including Cantonese and several other Chinese dialects. The films would supplement a course on safety rules. Crew members who passed the courses would be eligible to be certified as masters of safety and procedures. The certification had the added benefit of reducing the tankers' insurance costs. In order to boost our credibility, I hired two outside consultants. Captain Feldman had spent 40 years working on tankers; he had then served as director of all the tanker fleets for a major oil company. His job was to make sure every word and image related to shipboard safety were absolutely correct. Bob Demchuk, my other hire, was a young producer who had served in Vietnam and directed Army movies there. He'd also directed and produced *Sesame Street* projects, television specials, and commercials.

One night, almost 5 years after I'd been appointed president of Visual Library, Vera and I had dinner in Chinatown. It was a beautiful spring evening, and after dinner we took a walk through the narrow streets, crowded with people, and came upon a novelty store. We decided to look around, and I came across a cassette much smaller than the version we were using at Video Library Systems. I knew this would replace the present system we had, and make it easier for the fleets to become their own distributors, at a much lower cost. I told Vera we were heading home to Long Island and I would be taking off for London the next day.

As soon as my plane landed at Heathrow Airport, I headed straight to the offices of my British competitors. They weren't surprised by my unexpected visit, because I often stopped by to see them when I was in London. We gossiped about the tanker industry and which movies were getting the most orders. Then I casually mentioned the real reason for my trip. I'd just been diagnosed with a "health situation" that required my immediate attention. My family, friends, and colleagues were all very concerned because my situation would hamper my ability to continue as Chief Executive Officer of Video Library Systems.

My team of rivals put on a credible show of sympathy, but they could hardly hide their excitement. I could hardly hide my amusement. I tried not to laugh aloud, knowing they were already envisioning sole-source access to movie entertainment on worldwide fleets. I ate lunch, talked a bit more about my unnamed illness—serious but not fatal— and then off I went to check into my favorite hotel, the Royal Garden Hotel. Nobody mentioned the word "buyout" until the next day. By the end of the week, we had negotiated the terms and completed the paperwork. They thought they were getting the deal of their lives, so they acted quickly and didn't bother to do their...yes, it's called "due diligence." Once the deal was done, I booked a seat from Heathrow to New York. On my way across the Atlantic Ocean, I sipped on a glass of champagne as I silently toasted the restaurant in Chinatown that had been the first stop on my journey. I allowed myself a second glass in order to toast my English friends, who had shown such concern about my health.

One reason I was so eager to sell the company was that Video Library owned the 40,000 square-foot building in Greece, with 12 employees and all the equipment required to run the business. My fear was that my assets would soon be worth less than their book value, because the Greek economy was taking such a deep nosedive.

The Sale couldn't happen fast enough. Bob Demchuk had written a script about returning Vietnam's veterans. In 1946, the American people had greeted the World War II vets with open arms. Returning Vietnam Vets, on the other hand, were treated like second hand citizens. I wanted to do whatever I could to right the wrong. I told Bob that I would be honored to become his executive producer and raise the necessary funds to turn his script into a movie. As it turned out, I could have written my own movie about what happens when my middle-class, poker-playing pals envisioned themselves as Hollywood moguls.

***

Vera and I had moved to East Northport, Long Island, in 1953, soon after we got married. We lived in the same comfortable home for fifty years, and not once did we think about leaving. Our three sons and our daughter lived, loved, laughed, and cried there. It was a good house, a safe haven in a neighborhood overflowing with life.

When we moved to Long Island, our town was located near potato, strawberry, and duck farms, all of which are gone today. Most of our neighbors were World War II veterans and their wives, who were starting families and working hard to move up to the middle class, just as we were. We were very self-sufficient in those days. We did our own home repairs, mowed our own lawns, and did our best to support our local churches and synagogues. We developed strong relationships, and our families grew in size and deep affection for one another. We were living the American Dream: a house, a family, children, and lasting friendships. Every Friday night, sixteen or so men from the neighborhood would get together to play poker. We played for money, but the real prize was bragging rights for the week, much like the pigeon contests in Ozone Park. The only acceptable topics of conversation were the poker game, sports, movies, local politics, and the kids. Although many of the fellows had interesting jobs and professions, if any of them started to talk about work, somebody would inevitably yell, "Hey, lay down your cards! We're here to make some money!"

As the years went by, the players' lifestyles changed. Some of the men, myself included, had to travel often and far away. But when they returned home, they always sought the familiar comfort of the poker game. By then, the attendance on any given Friday night was usually no more than eight men. Talking about business was still banned, so I was caught off guard when I casually mentioned that I was going to be an executive producer for a movie called *Whatever It Takes*. The poker game immediately stopped, and the movie became the topic of conversation for the rest of the evening.

When I admitted I'd written a business plan, everyone wanted in. Neither Vera nor I wanted them to invest their money, because I'd never produced a movie, and I knew nothing about the process. We were afraid that if the movie failed, they would lose their hard-earned savings. We couldn't bear the thought of that happening to our dearest friends.

"The best way to become rich is to own a profitable business. But most of us don't have the time, expertise, or access to capital to start and run our own company," I reminded them. "Even if we do, most new businesses fail in the first few years, and I don't have any experience in the movie business."

They refused to listen. They wanted in.

The next Friday, they wanted to know how much it would cost to invest. I thought that reciting some numbers from the prospectus might scare them off. "The total capitalization of the partnership for the production company is $1,190,000. We're selling partnership interests in 35 units at $34,000 per unit."

I was wrong. Another Friday rolled around, and once again, all they wanted to discuss was the movie. "What did you say it's called? And what's it about?" one of them asked.

"*Whatever It Takes*. It's a romance, set in New York City, about a young man who comes back from Vietnam and wants to be a cartoonist instead of taking over his father's business. We want it to be both funny and touching."

"Walter, how did you get involved?" asked my neighbor who lived directly across the street.

"I wanted to do something to honor our veterans, because I didn't like that they were treated disrespectfully when they got back from Vietnam."

"Who's going to be in it? Anyone we've heard of?"

"Martin Balsam plays the father. He won an Oscar for best supporting actor in *A Thousand Clowns*." I reeled off the names of the other actors. "Chris Weatherhead, Lee Bickford, James Rebhorn, Rosetta LeNoire, Tom Mason, Maura Shea…"

Most of the guys shook their heads. They didn't get to see many movies. But they were digesting every word, and I could tell they wanted more. "We'll have seven new songs by Gary Sherman and Peter Udell. The two of them have written more than 30 top-ten hits."

By the time we were done talking about the movie, the evening was over. I don't think we played even one full hand. At least we saved our money!

Although Vera rarely had a cross word for me, she was very upset after everyone left. "You're encouraging them," she scolded me.

"I'm not," I protested. "They're determined to get involved."

Hoping to dissuade them, and to ease our consciences, I created an extremely onerous agreement, spelling out every single risk and consequence. I was sure they'd discuss it amongst themselves and return the document unsigned. I imagined the relief Vera and I would feel upon hearing, "I've thought it over. I'm sorry, but I can't sign this." I insisted they consult their lawyers—and more importantly, their wives. But to our dismay, they could not be swayed! Each one of the poker boys laid out thirty-five thousand dollars a unit. Some of them even insisted on buying two units!

The next time we met to play poker (if only), they were curious about the total cost of the movie. Making a movie is a major business operation, so I'd had to put together a prospectus for prospective investors, and also send a copy to the Securities and Exchange Commission for its approval.

"The major expenses will include over 200 individual contracts for services, as well as the cost of 90,000 square feet of film. The subtotal for just that comes to $643,802."

I kept piling on the numbers to persuade them that they couldn't afford to get involved.

"We have to buy an insurance policy for a million dollars, which will cost us $17,900. The hospital scene, which the director estimates will take four days to shoot, will cost $1,500 per day, and renting out a diner will cost $18,850. And this is a small-budget film!"

The numbers were shocking, even to me, and I'd gone over them so often I'd memorized them.

But the more I tried to discourage them, the more insistent they were, every single one of them, about investing in the movie. After all, they were poker players! The entire group eventually invested approximately $500,000, about half the total amount I had to raise. I knew this was an immense sacrifice for them, which felt extremely stressful for both Vera and me.

Now I really had to pray that the movie would be a success—at least successful enough to earn back what they'd invested.

The men and their wives met some of the cast and the songwriters. They were getting a huge kick out of their involvement in the process. They repeatedly announced to me—and Vera, who managed to keep smiling—that nothing as exciting had ever before happened to them.

They were amazed for the duration of the shoot, we'd been assigned our own New York City police detail.

My poker buddies sometimes had lunch or dinner with cast members or other celebrities, which was the highlight of their week, and the all-consuming topic of conversation that Friday night. No matter what was going on at work or home, they'd get so absorbed by what was happening on the set that they could forget reality and feel better...at least for a while.

After the last scene was shot, the whole poker crowd was invited to the wrap party, which marked the last time the entire cast and crew had a chance to hang out and celebrate a job well done. My friends felt honored to have been invited to such an emotional gathering.

The shoot was finished, but my work wasn't. I had to find a distributor, the person responsible for the up-front costs of promoting and marketing the film, making the reels, setting a release date, finding a movie theater or theaters. The distributor is also the first person to get reimbursed. First monies in are his...

I headed out to Hollywood to visit the major movie companies. As it turned out, my sole responsibility was to deliver the movie reels to wherever the studio's head of Marketing happened to be located.

I thought of all the newsreels I'd watched, in which the actor would drive up to the studio entrance and smile at the guard. "Hello, Mr. Gable," the guard would say, waving him through. "Go right ahead. They're expecting you."

I was sure that when I arrived at the studio, I'd get the same treatment. The guard would say, "Hello, Mr. Scherr. Go ahead, they're expecting you." And they did. I would drive around the lot to the sound stage and leave my three cans of reels there. I felt like a real VIP!

When I showed up at MGM and Universal Studios, I got the same response from the people I'd phoned ahead of time. "Walter, this movie needs legs." In movie speak that meant the movie had to open in several theaters on the same day, and it had to draw large and enthusiastic audiences for three or four weeks in a row. This made my job even harder!

Twentieth Century Fox was my last hope, but they gave me the same answer. I picked up my cans and drove back to my hotel. As I pulled up in front of the main entrance, I decided I didn't want to leave the cans unattended. But they were so heavy that I didn't want to park in the lot, which was about five minutes away from the hotel, then have to carry them all the way back. I stood by my car, trying to make up my mind and not feeling comfortable with either decision. Unbeknownst to me, I was being watched. When a couple of men ambled over, I did an actual, real-life double take. Standing in front of me were Telly and George Savalas, whom I instantly recognized from their roles in *Kojak*, one of my favorite television shows. "What's on your mind?" asked Telly, the older of the two. "You look so confused."

I explained my dilemma.

"Leave the cans here. We'll watch them for you," George said. I was astonished, relieved, and grateful. What a terrific story to tell the poker boys—Lieutenant Kojak and Sergeant Stavros guarding our film!

The next morning I came downstairs, and who was sitting in the dining room? Telly and George, surrounded by a crowd of family members, switching back and forth between English and Greek while they ate breakfast. As soon as they saw me, they invited me to join them. What was I doing in LA? George asked. I told them about my movie.

"That's not what you do with a small-budget movie," Telly said. "Go over to Sunset Strip. You'll see a bunch of small theaters that are specifically designed to show movies to distributors. They each have ten or fifteen seats. You rent one of those places, take out ads in *Variety* and *The Hollywood Reporter*, show your movie three times a day, and invite distributors."

"I think I know the right place," he said. He drove me over to Sunset Strip and introduced me to the theater owner. I rented the place for two weeks. I showed the movie, talked it up, gave flyers to anybody willing to take one, and still didn't get a distributor. Sometimes only two or three people showed up to see the movie.

Two days before the end of my second week, a man stood up at the end of the six o'clock show and came over to shake my hand. He said, "My name's Terry Levine. I know Bob Demchuk. I might be able to help you."

Terry told me he owned a couple of movie houses on 42nd Street in New York, and that he made martial arts movies. What he didn't mention was that he also made very graphic horror movies or that he'd earned millions of dollars by intercutting scenes from different movies and splicing them together to create a brand-new film. Terry owned a distribution company, Aquarius Films, and he had connections with 20th Century Fox.

The movie premiered at the Eastside Cinema in February 1986, one of the coldest days of the year in New York. The poker guys and I rented three buses and invited almost everyone we knew ... friends, family, neighbors, and the rest of the investors. It felt like New Year's Eve. My mother came and led the celebration!

One of the first things Terry did was secure a contract for all independent TV stations in the United States. This would give them the rights to show the movie, and enough cash funds would secure my investors' money. Seeing my name on the big screen ranks high on my list of great thrills. I felt immortalized forever—at least for a minute or two. I enjoyed getting to know everyone I worked with.

I wouldn't have thought so on those Friday evenings when we sat around the table, talking movies instead of playing poker, but I am thrilled to have shared that once-in-a-lifetime experience with my closest friends and neighbors. I'm also forever grateful that none of them lost any money. I cherish our bond, which grew even stronger during the months when the East Northport poker boys went Hollywood. We talked about our adventures in moviemaking for years afterward. It's a take!

BLACK GOLD

IN ORDER TO TELL YOU THE STORY OF WALTER J. SCHERR, OIL BARON—MAYBE the only one in the history of Ozone Park—I have to step back in time a little bit from where we just left off.

During two separate oil crises in the 1970s, Americans from coast to coast faced persistent gas shortages as OPEC flexed its muscles and disrupted oil supplies. 1979 was an especially rough year. Sheikh Ayatollah Khomeini had won the revolution in Iran and was appointed the dictatorial ayatollah of Iran, which had suddenly been transformed into an Islamic nation. Iran, an important supplier of oil to the United States, cut its oil "output" by almost five million barrels a day. The revolution in Iran triggered fears of similar conflicts in other Middle East countries.

By April 1979, the United States found itself in the middle of an oil shortage. President Carter described it as the "moral equivalent of war." Memories of the similar crisis in 1973 motivated "a sharp increase in precautionary demand." The price of oil kept rising, and the supplies kept falling. OPEC, the world's largest and most powerful oil export group, doubled the price of crude oil. Inflation soared in the United States, and gas reserves kept shrinking. If you were old enough to drive in those days, you remember waiting for hours at the gas station, where long lines of cars snaked around the block. The situation became a crisis when spring gave way to summer as Americans took to the highways for their vacations.

Customers were not above fighting over the lessening supplies of gas. In June, New York's Governor Hugh Carey instituted an "odd-even" system for New York City and four surrounding counties, including Nassau, Suffolk (which included my neighborhood), Westchester, and Rockland. Drivers had to purchase gas on alternating days, depending on whether they had odd- or even-numbered license plates. It wasn't long before New Jersey and Connecticut put in place the same rules.

I was angry. I resented the fact that we were so completely dependent on foreign oil. As a proud American citizen with a risk-taking entrepreneurial spirit, I had a bucket list that included a plan to get involved in the energy business. My dream was that someday my family could help the United States become self-sufficient in the area of energy.

My oldest son, Doug, majored in accounting and taught in a high school for several years. He then earned an MBA and got a job in the accounting and contracts department at Grumman Aircraft.

My second son, Walter III, whom everyone calls Bud, developed such a strong interest in geology that during his junior year in college, he was part of a team that traveled to the North Pole. He studied to be a petroleum engineer, and after he graduated, he was employed at a major oil company.

During the twelve years he worked for that company, Bud got to know a great deal about the oil business. He also earned his MBA. Unfortunately, the downturn in the economy in the 1980s left the larger oil companies with no other choice than to offer compensation packages to those who opted to leave the company. I knew that with Bud's unique experiences, we could become part of an industry that would one day be self-sufficient in the United States.

I made the decision to risk the family's assets, and we established Valence Operating, an oil and gas exploration company. Bud became a partner with John Averhoff, a senior petroleum engineer. Douglas then relocated to Texas from New York with his expertise in finance. They were soon joined by another senior petroleum engineer, Steve Manning. The three engineers—Bud, John, and Steve—each had 15 years' experience in the oil and gas business. The team was supported by the Board of Directors: Haskew Brantley, Arlindo Jorge, Dave Black, and myself. All associated with the company including their families had "skin in the game." When we started Valence, crude oil was selling at $20 a barrel, a little more than $1 per gallon of regular gas. Natural gas was also low, so there wasn't much incentive to dig and produce it. Most people wouldn't have chosen to start in that business during that time, but I believe that sometimes it's good to go into something when the risk-reward ratio can pay big dividends.

We had an ambitious long-range plan. One of our goals, which we still believe will come to fruition within the next twenty years, was to develop the technology to convert diesel engines, which now use only oil, into a dual-fuel engine that uses both oil and natural gas. These changes would result in the United States no longer being dependent on foreign oil.

In our first three years, we were successful in purchasing wells that were producing below 100 barrels a day from major oil companies like Exxon, Mobil, and Texaco. We increased output by 30 to 40 percent with care and cutting-edge industry techniques. Eventually we ventured into drilling wells ourselves. This was much riskier and more expensive; failure of the wells to produce could mean failure of the company.

The first well we drilled turned into a life-threatening and potential financial disaster. This created a make-or-break situation for the company. The well was in a flood zone, and it had begun to rain nonstop. The water was rising higher and higher, and so was the risk. Our well, which had started out about 10 feet above the water level, ended up 10 feet below water level. To make matters worse, our lease (the rights to the minerals) would soon expire. It was mandatory we get the well into production within the week.

The first strategy that we thought of was to wait and see whether the water level could be controlled by a dam, which would then cause the water to diminish enough to put the well into production before the lease ran out. I received a phone call from my son informing me that the dam option would not work. We simply did not have enough time for that. He told me that the prospect for a producing well was just not in the cards and that nature had upset our plans. I told him that failure was not an option; that we had to think creatively to come up with something that would save our family's financial condition. We had come this far and I wasn't taking no for an answer.

We had everything planned out perfectly by the best of the best in the industry...except the weather. I knew it was a risk going in, but I had so much hope that I had disregarded the "what ifs"?

As if the situation weren't bad enough, a huge cold front brought on winter conditions, and the lake that had formed over our well froze. It was perfect for an ice skating rink but not for oil well drilling. The good news was that we had an "out of the box" solution that was proposed. The bad news was that Bud, and his partner John, had to dive under the ice to fix the problem themselves, with the help of Steve Manning, a consultant and expert scuba diver.

I said to Bud, "Are you out of your ever-loving minds?"

I could never forgive myself if something went wrong down there. But I knew we had run out of options.

I had not only my family's future at stake, but also those of my many friends and colleagues. I felt as if I had the weight of the world on my shoulders. As I listened to their plan, I realized we had no other choice.

We decided to go ahead with the plan, to descend through the thick layers of ice, into the freezing cold lake waters. Before we could proceed, Bud and John had to learn how to scuba dive! They would have to squeeze in just enough lessons to learn safe diving procedures. I spoke to Bud after every class. He sounded confident and upbeat. I had to ignore the impulse to call off the whole project.

The day of reckoning finally came. They rented the necessary gear, and they informed emergency personnel to stand by for assistance. They dove through the small hole that was carved out of the ice, into the freezing water. My nerves were all over the place. I couldn't stand still, and my stomach was in knots. I realized they were risking their lives for the benefit of the family, our friends, and our country.

When I finally got word that it had worked, and I realized they were safe, I breathed a huge sigh of relief! They had successfully hooked up the well underwater. The boys were heroes. The company stayed in business, and the goal of energy independence was now one huge step closer.

Since that time, my family's company has continued to explore new technologies to extract more and more oil from the ground, and with minimal impact to our precious environment. Our first well resulted in a 1,540-foot horizontal well with three distinct fracks, approximately 500 feet apart. At this writing, we have just completed a well with a 10,000-foot horizontal displacement and 38 individual fractures. This is a good example of how technology has improved over the last 15 years, and how individual entrepreneurs have moved the industry forward in a way that, in my opinion, government planners never could.

I know many Americans are very unhappy with the oil companies, and sometimes for reasons I can sympathize with. On the other hand, it's simplistic and wrong to always characterize the oil industry as the bad guy. As this book is being written, the oil and gas industry in the United States is engaged in an epic struggle to maintain its goal of energy independence. The shale revolution ensured that by 2020, the United States would no longer be dependent on foreign oil. But foreign interests have declared a price war on the United States' oil and gas industry.

Although the United States' oil industry might suffer greatly from this, everything else will benefit because of the "cap" on the price of oil and gas from foreign producers. Not only will other industries benefit from this, but it will raise the world's standard of living, thanks in large part to the efforts of American oil and gas entrepreneurs.

Retirement, Heck No! Technology Revolution, Heck Yes!

Almost everyone I know loves chocolate cake. A great chocolate cake is usually not just a treat. It's a comfort food that brings back memories—of childhood, of special times like birthdays or parties when the family or good friends gathered around the table. Vera made a chocolate cake that everyone loved. Al Busching, an old friend from Sperry, couldn't get enough of it. Little did I know that Vera's chocolate cake would lead me into the exciting arena of the high-tech revolution.

One day in 1987, not long after *Whatever It Takes* appeared in theaters, and I had sold Video Library Systems, I was driving north on Glen Cove Road and stopped to get gas.

"Hey!" I heard someone call out. "Is Vera still making that delicious chocolate cake?"

I immediately recognized the voice; it belonged to none other than Al, who had pulled up to the pumps on the southbound side of the station. We threw our arms around each other like long-lost brothers. At Sperry, we had shared an office, a secretary, and a lot of good times.

Thirty years had passed, and we both looked a bit older, but otherwise nothing had changed. We chatted for a few minutes about our families and what we were doing. Al was the chief executive officer of Veeco Lambda, a major worldwide technology company headquartered on Long Island. He laughed when I told him about *Whatever It Takes* and my foray into movie producing.

"So you've gone Hollywood?" he said, shaking his head in disbelief.

"Once was enough," I assured him.

I told him I was on my way to a financial seminar at the Nassau Country Club.

"Hey, I have something you can do for me," he said. "You've bought and sold a lot of companies. We're thinking of buying a company on Long Island, but we need someone like you to look it over." The company Al had in mind, UPA Technology, manufactured x-ray machines with a wide range of military and industrial uses. He needed someone to perform the due diligence: to examine UPA's financials and analyze whether they were in order.

The other factor to consider was whether UPA would be a good fit for Veeco Lambda. Every company has its own particular culture, and when the cultures clash, the merger suffers. Whenever I contemplated an acquisition, I had to be sure that one and one would equal three. If you think my math is wrong, consider this: A successful acquisition has to achieve the following: a) increased sales and profits for the benefit of shareholders; b) expansion of the company's technical capabilities; and c) advancement of the company's long-term strategic goals.

The Greek philosopher, Aristotle, said it first and best: "The whole is greater than the sum of its parts." Whether you call it synergy, which comes from the Greek word for "working together," or teamwork, companies with compatible objectives and employees can expand more quickly than a single company working on its own.

At the risk of sounding as if I'm boasting, I was the perfect person for Al's job. I knew what to look for when evaluating a company; I'd been doing it for thirty-plus years. I spent the next five months checking out UPA: their income statements and balance sheets; their product lines; their executives and the people who worked on the factory floor. Then I sat down with Al and the rest of the Board and told them that UPA was an excellent match for Veeco Lambda. UPA's product line fit right in with Veeco Lambda's, which would make for great synergy.

"Walter, you did a great job," Al said. "If you like UPA so much, why don't you stay here and run it?" I accepted his offer.

It was *bashert*, the Yiddish word for fate, destiny, something that was meant to be. Another definition for bashert is "an excellent match."

I was 62, and a lot of my friends were happily planning for their retirement. But I welcomed the challenge of running a new company, especially one that was part of Veeco Lambda. The chairman of the board, Albert Nerken, had studied chemistry at Cooper Union, a full-scholarship private university in New York's East Village. During World War II, he and another chemist, Frank Raible, had worked together on the Manhattan Project, creating systems to prevent leaks from contaminating the uranium for the atomic bomb.

After the war, the two men moved to Long Island and founded the Vacuum Electronic Engineering Company, which produced helium leak detectors and high-vacuum equipment. The company was renamed Veeco Lambda in 1965, when they acquired Lambda Electronics, which manufactured current converters and other power supplies for industrial and military clients.

Sidney Lieber, the founder and head of UPA at that time, was a very warm and genuine person whom I was fortunate to get to know. Many of his employees, who had started at UPA right after college, had worked there for ten or more years. Sid was a brilliant engineer and inventor. He had built his company from scratch, but he was much more of a scientist than an executive. He was a fascinating man, and whenever we chatted, I always walked away feeling as if he'd shared a lot of wisdom and good advice with me. Sid didn't "manage" people; he treated everyone in the company like family, and they all adored him.

A corporate acquisition is like a marriage. It takes hard work and diplomacy to blend two very separate cultures into a productive—and happy—union. In the very funny movie, *Meet the Parents*, Ben Stiller plays Greg Focker, a nervous fiancé meeting his prospective in-laws for the first time. Robert DeNiro plays Jack Byrnes, the suspicious father and ex-CIA agent who eyeballs Stiller as if he's an enemy spy. Jack, who suspects Greg of trying to infiltrate his family in order to steal his beloved daughter, will stop at nothing to undermine Greg's efforts.

I'm sure that many of the people at UPA felt that I was the enemy, infiltrating and trying to radically change their company. Long-time employees are like a close-knit family who accept their ideas and idiosyncrasies. The UPA people had to adjust themselves to a new head guy, someone whose background and ideas were different from theirs. I could guess what they were feeling: Who is this guy? How are we supposed to work with a total stranger? He doesn't know anything about us or our company. Their feelings were natural. Experience told me I had to be patient and reassure them that I could add value to the company, make it grow, which would increase the value of their experience and their compensation.

As was the case when I was sent to London by Sperry nearly 30 years earlier, my major task was to change the culture. On my first day at Veeco, I assigned manufacturing management the task of producing within one month a "defective parts" report by product, scheduled to be complete in one month. I also issued a memo to all employees that a mandatory breakfast meeting would be held the day after the parts report was due. At the meeting, I introduced the 80/20 rule which I had followed so successfully in earlier endeavors. I announced that this formula would be applied across the board, including accounts receivable, accounts payable, inventory, purchasing, engineering, etc. We handed out the defective parts report at the meeting to all our employees. Just as I had anticipated, the report identified that 20 percent of the defective parts were responsible for 80 percent of the problems. My point was that their inability to meet the schedule or complete a job should not be part of the crucial 20 percent.

The next rule I announced is another one I've followed throughout my career. It's best described as the 3-in-1 egg theory. Every egg consists of the yellow, the white, and the shell. If one of those ingredients isn't in proportion to the others, it will be a rotten egg. Same in business. The priorities of the employees, the stockholders, and the customers all have to be in balance. If one element becomes misaligned, the two other elements will suffer, and worse case scenario, you end up with a rotten company.

At Veeco, we had a strategic five to ten-year plan to make sure we didn't lay an egg. Included in that plan was hiring and promoting the right kind of talent to ensure a strong management team. We were fortunate to find some top people who shared my view that in the business world, every adversity offers opportunity. As a result, we were able to reimburse Lambda Veeco within 15 months the money they invested to purchase UPA. We proceeded to have a growth rate of about 30 percent a year.

In 1988, Unitech, a British company, expressed strong interest in buying Veeco. Mr. Nerken, by then in his mid-seventies and still serving as chairman of the board, wanted to retire, and Unitech's offer of more than $250 million persuaded him to sell. We soon realized that although Unitech had purchased all of Veeco's divisions, they were only interested in Lambda. It was a matter of synergy: both Unitech and Lambda sold power supplies and connectors. Veeco was an afterthought, as far as the Brits were concerned, and those of us in management were concerned about the fate of Mr. Nerken's company. As Veeco Instrument's chief operating officer, Ed Braun, on behalf of Veeco's senior management, myself included, made an offer in 1989 to buy back the Veeco Instrument Group from Unitech. We hadn't lined up the funding to buy the company, but Unitech gave us time to raise the money—$29.2 million. It took us a year to create our business plan. Now we had to find our investors.

Chemical Bank, which had been Veeco Lambda's bank for years, knew we had enough equipment to collateralize the loan. But they also wanted to see that we had "skin in the game." In other words, they expected each of us to add our own money to the pot.

Everyone who was part of the management team—Dick Baglio, Bob Oates, Francis Steenbeke, Ed, and I—had to contribute to the equity loan. Rich d'Amore, a strategic genius and a gem of a fellow, also invested as an equity partner on behalf of Hambro International Equity Partner; he therefore was appointed to Veeco's Board of Directors. Mr. Nerken also became a major shareholder, because he wanted to continue his association with the company.

I had money from the sale of Video Library Systems, which I had earmarked for my retirement. I was so certain that Veeco Instrument Group (or "New Veeco," as we came to call it) would succeed that I was willing to take a chance. Of course, I talked to Vera about it, but she had faith in me, especially after we had survived the Matsushita disaster. It was a different story for the other fellows. Aside from Ed, none of them had the kind of nest egg that I did. Nevertheless, they felt so confident that their initial reaction was, "No problem. I'm the man of the house. I can get you the money by Friday." And then they went home and talked to their wives.

Over the next several days, they each came into my office looking sheepish and embarrassed. It was as if they were all reading from the same script: "Walter, why don't you come for dinner next week? How's Wednesday? Or Thursday? How do you feel about spaghetti?"

I felt fine about spaghetti. I understood their problem. Some of them would have to refinance their houses. Others would have to contribute their life savings. Their wives might have met me two or three times at a company picnic or party. Even if they'd heard good things about me from their husbands, they'd be taking a huge risk. They had kids in high school or younger. What if our venture didn't work out? How would they to pay their mortgage? Where would they get the money for their kids' college education?

They'd raised a lot of "what if" and worst-case scenarios, and all of them were real. I had to do one of the best sell jobs of my life. I've always been good at marketing, but this was different. This was personal. They all had nice homes on Long Island, homes they'd worked hard to pay for. They were very hospitable, and the food was delicious. But they didn't try to hide their concern while they listened to me. I made it clear that each family had to make its own decision. I didn't want anyone's "yes" on my conscience. "It's very rare that you get an opportunity to invest in this type of company at a price with such a high rate of return, assuming the investment comes to realization. We're on the edge of a revolution," was what I explained, between forkfuls of rigatoni or mashed potatoes. "In a few years, you'll see new technology that you can't even imagine today. For industry and consumers. If we get involved now, we'll eventually reap the rewards."

Yes, they were taking a risk, I acknowledged. But sometimes you have to be a risk-taker. And this was a once-in-a-lifetime chance to become financially independent.

These women were smart and savvy. They asked a lot of questions, and I was completely honest with them. "I don't want to put you on the spot," I said. "Talk it over, talk to your kids if that feels right to you. But I need to know soon, as soon as possible."

I came home night after night and looked at my house and wondered what Vera and I would do if we were in the same situation. I had to believe we'd say, as all the other couples did, "Yes, we're in!" The response I got from every one of them is what distinguishes the entrepreneur from someone who's afraid to take a risk.

Francis Steenbeke, Veeco's head of International Sales and Marketing, owned a home in France. He'd bought a beautiful piece of property near his house that he would have to put on the market in order to raise his share of equity. "Before I sell, you have to come to France and look at it, so you'll know what I'm sacrificing," he said. I went to see it, and it was beautiful. Francis sold the property so he could invest in Veeco. He never regretted his decision.

In order to secure our loan from Chemical Bank, three separate departments—bonds, loans, and equity—had to agree to lend us money. The loans department lent us $10 million; the equity department agreed to accept company stock worth $10 million. But the woman in charge of the bonds department refused to commit to our request. She fascinated us: In 1990, very few women were in charge of powerful banking departments, but she was very smart and an excellent businesswoman. She was young, only in her thirties, and very attractive. We called her "Fur Coat Banker," because she wore a different fur coat every time we met with her. She was in charge of the last $10 million we desperately needed, and she didn't seem in a hurry to lend it to us. But time was of the essence. I was sure that within a couple of weeks, the banks would no longer take the risk of financing any new ventures. Without the $30 million we hoped to borrow, we couldn't afford to finance our management buyout of Veeco. Fur Coat Banker seemed to enjoy watching us beg and plead with her. She would frequently make appointments with Ed and me, and cancel them at the last minute. She scheduled a meeting for the three of us—at 8 o'clock on a Friday evening! Strange timing, but we didn't care. We were so desperate by then that we would have showed up at two in the morning. Ed and I were experienced businessmen, who'd encountered all kinds of challenging situations. But that evening, we were almost shaking with anxiety when we arrived at her office in downtown New York. Eight o'clock came and went, but Fur Coat Banker was a no-show. We waited and waited and waited, and still she didn't appear.

At ten o'clock, we finally left her office. The trip back to Long Island gave us plenty of time to fume and rage. We had all kind of theories to explain her behavior. She was deliberately tormenting us! She wanted to prove that she was the queen, and we were the lowly peasants who had to come begging! We were prepared to beg. If she didn't give us a loan, the rest of the money would disappear.

"We can't wait until Monday to see her," I told Ed. "You have to get us in there this weekend!"

Ed agreed. We were both shocked when she said she could see us on Sunday at 9 a.m. As usual, we arrived early. I told Ed that we'd go into her office together. I would summarize our financial position and remind Fur Coat Banker how much we needed. Then I'd excuse myself and give Ed a chance to talk to her one-on-one. "You're the CEO, so it's up to you to close this deal," I said.

"'Whatever it takes,' to quote your favorite movie," he said.

Fur Coat Banker arrived fifteen minutes late, but at least she arrived. I gave her a succinct but thorough explanation of our fiscal situation. I told her why we needed her help: that a loan from her department would enable us to successfully move forward in our market. She seemed to listen carefully, and she took lots of notes.

After I made my final point, I said, "I'm going to wait outside. The two of you can work out the details."

I paced the anteroom as I waited for Ed. I imagined him using his considerable charm to persuade her to close the deal. After the longest hour I'd ever spent, the office door finally opened. Ed held up a signed contract for $10 million dollars and winked at me. "Let's go," he said.

I didn't ask—and he never told me—what he said or did to get that contract or what arrangements they made. It didn't matter.

We were finally able to buy the company in early 1990, just as the world economy was plunging into a downturn. At the end of the year, our balance sheet showed five times more debt than equity. We had $25 million in sales, but we were $30 million in debt. For the first few years, Veeco's mission was to generate cash in order to live another day. We constantly struggled to make payroll and avoid debt default. Those were very tough times. The management team took a big pay cut, and all the employees, except for management, went to a four-day workweek. But I never doubted we had done the right thing. I had no time for regrets, because I was too busy paying the bills and making sure we could always make payroll. The consultants we spoke to tried to convince us to file for bankruptcy, but we were determined to make a success of the Veeco Instrument Group. If we had filed for bankruptcy, we would have missed out on the most important opportunity of the 20th century, participating in the development of the emerging high-tech industry.

My friends and family, many of whom were retired, thought I was crazy to continue working. I was over 65, and I already had enough money without my Veeco salary to maintain our comfortable lifestyle. People close to me wondered why I was working so hard, fighting what they considered a losing battle.

What they didn't understand was that I was doing exactly what I enjoyed most. I loved feeling challenged, and saving Veeco was definitely a challenge. I had promised our stockholders, employees, and vendors that Veeco would become a profitable venture. I couldn't walk away from my obligations. And I was very fortunate to be part of a great team. We all agreed that failure was not an option.

Rich D'Amore and Ed envisioned the company realigning itself to become a technology company focused on supplying capital equipment to semiconductor data storage and scientific industries. We knew we had bought what amounted to a "one-trick pony"; the company's inventory consisted primarily of leak detection systems and high-vacuum equipment, similar to those sold by Veeco's original founders. Our plan was to provide service and parts for the 20,000 units of equipment that we had in the field, and use the profits to expand into more lucrative areas by developing state-of-the-art technology. As with any company just starting out, we had our ups and down—and some weeks it felt as if we had more downs than ups.

I remember one Friday night, sitting with Bob Oates, Veeco's Treasurer, trying to figure out how we could collect enough money by Wednesday to pay our employees on time. We decided I would call the president of a company in San Francisco that made electronic components. The company hadn't yet paid for equipment they'd purchased from us because they claimed it didn't meet their specifications. I planned to ask the president to pay us only enough to make the payroll. When I got him on the phone, I explained that we were pushing the envelope of state-of-the art equipment, and that our product would make his product the gemstone of the industry. We needed to cooperate for long-range planning, I told him, and I'd appreciate his help with a partial payment. But the president wasn't buying my admittedly weak story. Until the equipment fully met the specs, he wouldn't pay us a dime. Like a dog with a bone, I couldn't give up. I promised that our top engineers would be at his plant on Monday morning to implement all the necessary adjustments. I heard a click, and then a dial tone.

"That SOB just hung up on me!"

"Calm down," Bob said. "I have a plan."

He had talked to friends in San Francisco and found out that the president played golf every Sunday at one of the city's most exclusive country clubs. He planned to show up at the club on Sunday and track down the company president and his golf buddies. "Desperate times, desperate measures," Bob said. "I'm not leaving until he hands over the rest of the money we need to pay our employees."

Bob's idea was so wacky that I would have started to laugh if I hadn't been so upset. I reminded him that the president could have him arrested for invading private property. "I'll do my best not to get arrested," he said. "But you better be damn sure you have the name and number of a lawyer out there. I'll do almost anything to keep this company alive, but I don't want to end up in jail."

We both poured ourselves a Scotch. I raised my glass to toast his success. "Here's to a great game of golf that doesn't end in the slammer."

Bob called me on Sunday afternoon to report that the company president had promised to send us a check on Monday, and by the way, I owed him a bottle of 12-year-old single malt Scotch. When my office phone rang at nine a.m. on Monday, I was sure Bob was calling to gloat about his success and to remind me what brand of Scotch he preferred. I was grinning as I picked up the phone and said, "I bet you're feeling pretty good this morning."

"It's six o'clock here," growled our customer in San Francisco. "I've been up since five, thinking about the nerve of that guy, Bob Oates, showing up at my club. I've been in business for umpteen years, but I've never met anyone with balls as big as you guys! The next time one of you shows up at my club, I'll have him arrested and thrown in jail."

"I totally understand," I said. All I got was the hum of the dial tone.

Meeting our payroll wasn't the only crisis we faced in those early years. We were constantly trying to figure out how to meet the bank covenants. We were hunkered down one afternoon in the office of Dick Baglio, Veeco's controller, worrying about our financial statements, which looked even worse than usual that month. We had a meeting the next day with our loan officers at Chemical Bank, and Dick would have to explain why we were defaulting on some of the covenants.

By the end of the next week, we would receive three overdue payments, which would put us into a non-default status. But as soon as we admitted to Chemical that we didn't have the money, our loan officers could take severe corrective action. We needed a miracle—or a creative solution.

I turned to Dick and said, "What are you doing here? Don't you have to deal with that emergency in Germany?"

Dick stared at me for a moment, and then he nodded. "Germany, right! I forgot about that."

"You better call your wife," I said.

We listened while Dick informed his wife that he had to fly to Germany that night because a problem had suddenly come up, and he was the only one of us who could deal with it. The conversation went on for a while; his wife obviously wasn't buying his story. We managed to control ourselves until he slammed down the phone and glared at us. "I'm in big trouble."

We laughed so hard we were falling out of our chairs. Pretty soon, Dick was laughing, too.

The next day, I had a clear conscience when I called the people at Chemical Bank. We were very sorry, I told them, but Dick was dealing with an emergency in Germany, and he was the person who was most familiar with the numbers. We rescheduled the meeting, and when we got together with them, we had no trouble proving that we could meet all our covenants.

We worked hard during those years, but we were a great team, and we had a lot of fun. We were like a bunch of cowboys, always ready to explore new territory and use every trick we knew to stay alive to fight another day. And after fifty years in business, I knew plenty of tricks.

One afternoon, at age 79, Mr. Nerken fell down in the middle of a game of tennis and was rushed to the hospital. We all expected to see him back in the office in a day or two. Then came the devastating news that he had been diagnosed with cancer, and it was terminal.

When we found ourselves in the midst of another financial crisis, this one so desperate that we had to refinance our debt, I didn't know what to tell him. I thought about all the years he'd spent creating and nurturing Veeco. The company was his baby, and he'd trusted us to take care of it and keep it going. I decided he needed to know what was happening, so I went over to his house and greeted him as usual. Then, because I was too nervous to make small talk, I plunged right in. I told him that Veeco was in danger of defaulting, and that we had put in as much money as we could, I hated to ask him for more, but...

Before I could finish my sentence, Mr. Nerken held up his hand. He called out for his wife to come into the room and asked her to bring his checkbook. He handed me a check for as much as was required to improve our financial condition and to keep going forward, and said with a smile, "I love this company."

Albert Nerken died in July 1992. The last time I visited him shortly before his death, he said that he wanted me to have the rocking chair in his office where he'd spent so much time. I used that rocking chair for the next 20 years until retirement.

In 1993, Ed Braun was appointed chairman of Semiconductor Equipment and Materials International, the trade association for our industry. Accepting such a prestigious position would be time consuming for Ed, but it was too good an opportunity for him to pass up. It also benefited Veeco, because a big part of his job was promoting our industry and talking about its future. When he was busy with SEMI business, I would handle his responsibilities.

One of my first assignments was to negotiate a deal with a Japanese company for a very large order of data storage products. Their chief financial officer and in-house auditors wanted to see our financials. We knew that as soon as they looked at our numbers, they would immediately lose interest in doing business with us. After many hours of discussion and lost sleep, I finally decided I'd meet with them. They wanted documentation, so I'd show them a document—although not the document they were expecting to see. I'd made hundreds of oral presentations and taught almost as many classes. If I could do one thing well, it was to speak without notes for as long as my audience was willing to listen. My plan was to start talking and keep on going until they were willing to sign anything, just to shut me up. What the heck? It was worth a try.

I walked into the boardroom at the company's headquarters in Tokyo and was introduced to the chief auditor and his management team. I tried to look confident and relaxed as the interpreter explained I had prepared some explanatory remarks. But when I glanced at the stern-faced chief auditor, I wondered how I could have dreamed up such a crazy scheme.

The men seated around the table expected me to give them a detailed statement of Veeco's financial status. All I had in my briefcase was the first page of the auditors' report from Veeco's most recent filing with the SEC. The title at the top of the page stated in big, bold letters: AUDITOR'S REPORT, followed by the name of our auditing firm. The text below declared in standard accounting language that they, our auditors, had examined Veeco's balance sheet in accordance with accepted accounting standards, that the statements, which reflected Veeco's financial position and any changes to its financial position, conformed to acceptable accounting practices. And on and on, without one substantive fact about our actual financial position.

I began to talk and kept on going, barely stopping to take a breath. My interpreter tried to keep up with me, but I could tell he was losing the race. I reached into my briefcase, pulled out the one-page document, and placed it in the middle of the table. The chief auditor grabbed it and put on his reading glasses. He looked at the title at the top of the page and readjusted his glasses. I stopped watching him and kept on talking. I didn't stop even after the chief auditor started screaming. I understood enough Japanese to know he was also cursing at me, using expressions not normally heard in a Tokyo boardroom.

I had to go to Plan B, which came to me in the midst of the auditor's rant. I turned to the company president, whom I'd met with briefly before the meeting. He'd told me in English good enough that we'd spoken without an interpreter that he knew about Veeco because he'd just attended a meeting of the Japanese semiconductor association. Ed Braun had been the main speaker. "A very big man," he'd said, obviously referring not to Ed's physical stature but to his importance in the semiconductor industry.

I leaned over to him and said, loudly enough that he could hear me above his auditor's harangue, "This isn't useful. Could we go somewhere else and speak?"

As the president ushered me out of the room, I imagined the auditor lunging across the table and pinning me to the floor in a wrestling hold.

"I apologize," the president said, once we'd escaped the sound of his auditor's rage. "He doesn't know about Ed Braun."

I nodded. That was exactly my point. The president knew about Ed Braun, and he therefore knew about Veeco. "These accounting details are very confusing," I said. "And I apologize if there's any misunderstanding. But since you've met Ed...." I wasn't sure they'd even been introduced, but the more we imagined, the better it would be for Veeco.

"Yes," said the president. "A very big man. Very smart."

"Very smart," I agreed. "That's why he's the CEO of Veeco. And also my very good friend."

The president smiled and shook my hand. Ed Braun's very good friend was a man he could trust. And Veeco had to be a very important company, worth many millions of dollars, because Ed Braun was, as we'd both agreed, "a very big man."

That's all he needed to know. He put the order through immediately, which gave us the infusion of capital that we needed to propel us forward. He invited me to have dinner with him that evening. The chief auditor would not be joining us.

***

Veeco was stuck in a Catch-22 situation: In order to acquire more money to expand, we needed to go public. In order to go public, we needed a product line that would capture the imagination of the financial community. Veeco's vacuum equipment was old-school technology, and we couldn't depend on it to build a powerhouse publicly traded company. As we knew, we needed at least two more horses in our stable. Sweeping innovations, comparable in scope to those of the Industrial Revolution, were giving birth to new companies that specialized in digital technology. Given our in-house talent and experience, we knew we could be leaders in the field of data storage. We were searching for a product that would fit our company's expertise. Francis Steenbeke, our long-time head of European operations, had an excellent eye for technology which he used to our advantage during his frequent meetings with European customers. While visiting one of our French clients, he stopped by their lab and noticed what he recognized as an early prototype of a data storage unit. He called and told us this could be the real deal, and we needed to jump on it before someone else did. If Francis was interested, we were interested. We gave him the green light to negotiate licensing rights to develop the concept from half-baked idea into a marketable disk drive. Our technical staff took it from partly conceived idea to a working disk drive, ready for mass production and sales.

Seagate Technology, one of the world's foremost manufacturers of hard disk drives, was our biggest account. We supplied them with ion beam etching equipment, an essential component of their HDD's, which they could not have produced without our expertise. Seagate comprised almost a third of our sales before our IPO at the end of 1994, a major increase from nine percent just two years earlier. But we still needed a another major product before we felt ready to take Veeco public.

We found it through serendipity—a lucky fluke, or maybe, if you're like me and don't believe in coincidence, another example of something that was *bashert*. One of our top salesmen, Roger, was visiting IBM's desktop computer factory in Boca Raton, Florida, when he noticed a group of engineers working off to the side on an atomic force microscope, an AFM. Two IBM scientists had developed the scanning tunneling microscope, the forerunner of the AFM, in 1981; five years later, they received the Nobel Prize in Physics for their invention. We were all familiar with the AFM, which allowed for the examination of materials on an atomic level and had many applications, including data storage.

As soon as Roger returned to our Long Island headquarters, he came into my office. "Walter, you won't believe what I just saw in Boca," he said. "There's about fifty engineers down there, working on an AFM, trying to improve its mass production. But I'll be damned if they know how to sell it."

We both had the same thought. Wow! The AFM was a very big deal, a very glamorous product. How the heck could our little company become involved in selling it?

Roger got a dreamy look on his face. "Walter, if we could get hold of it, this is our future."

Our future couldn't happen fast enough. I took the first flight to Boca Raton, zipped over to the IBM factory, and introduced myself to the AFM engineers. I told them all about Veeco and Albert Nerken; how our management team worked (deleting our most creative business solutions); our worldwide marketing capability, and whatever else I thought might impress them. IBM owned an almost permanent position on *Fortune* magazine's list of the world's top 100 companies. My presentation had the same effect on the engineers of "Big Blue" as if I were a pesky fly buzzing waiting to be squashed.

When my pitch failed to impress them, I asked Ed to come down and help me out. He was very personable, and also an expert on marketing as well as technology. He told them that Veeco had worldwide marketing, sales, and service capability. We had our own employees in Japan, Korea, Singapore, Mexico, and Europe. We threw ourselves into cultivating relationships with those engineers. We spent six months learning what their interests and hobbies were, whether they were married and had kids. We gave them VIP treatment, and they began to take us more seriously.

The chief engineer loved to go fishing. I've never understood the appeal of fishing: sitting in a boat for hours on end, no matter whether it's 95 degrees and the sun is beating down, or the sky is gray with storm clouds. All you can do is wait and hope some darn fish will swim by and take a bit of your bait. But if the head of that project wanted to go fishing, I'd import Jack and Ed and Francis, and a couple of other Veeco guys who liked to fish. We'd rent a boat for the day, head out to the Atlantic Ocean, and throw out our lines. And when the fish weren't biting, which they usually weren't, we'd talk about engineering, manufacturing, and sales. The chief engineer always had a huge smile on his face when he reeled in a fish. Meanwhile, we were doing our best to reel him in, and in the end, we all got what we wanted.

Compared to IBM, we were just a tiny speck of a company, but we presented an impressive array of capabilities: product development, quality control, distribution, sales, and marketing. In February 1993, IBM and Veeco Instruments signed an agreement that gave Veeco exclusive worldwide rights to market and service the AFM workstation. We had our second horse. We could finally take our company public.

We completed our initial public offering on December 6, 1994, trading on Nasdaq. Our net was 27.5 million dollars, which allowed us to repay our debt and use the rest of the capital for corporate improvement, as well as to move forward with our plan to expand in the area of high-precision instruments. John Rein, Jr., better known as "Jack," had replaced me as CFO in 1993, when I was diagnosed with cancer. I continued working at Veeco while I was undergoing treatments, but instead of remaining involved with day-to-day financial operations, I concentrated on researching and acquiring new companies. Quite a few years had passed since my years at Litton, where I'd learned how to research and evaluate companies with an eye toward acquisitions. I enjoyed the change in responsibilities; I also appreciated keeping busy, instead of turning into a cranky old man with nothing better to do than complain about my ill health.

High-tech industries were booming. The dot-com bubble was soaring higher and higher. For the first time since our management buyout in 1990, we had more profit than debt. What an exciting time it was in Veeco's history—and in my life, in spite of having to contend with cancer, followed by quadruple bypass surgery, and carotid artery disease. (Spoiler alert: I survived all three. No ghostwriter for *Walter's Way*.)

With the infusion of cash we received from taking Veeco public, we decided we could attract many more clients if we owned the manufacturing rights for the AFM, as well as the distribution rights. However, IBM informed us that they were in the midst of litigation with the person who owned the manufacturing patent rights. They couldn't negotiate anything with us until the case was settled, and then only if it was settled in their favor.

We wanted to meet this person who stood in the way of our progress. Virgil Elings, who'd earned a PhD at MIT, was a brilliant scientist, entrepreneur, and civic-minded philanthropist. After teaching physics at University of California at Santa Barbara for twenty years, he left in 1987 to co-found Digital Instruments, Inc. We decided we would solve our problem by purchasing Digital Instruments, which would then make Veeco the patent's owner. It seemed like an excellent solution, until I heard from a colleague at IBM that several other companies had approached Virgil about a merger. But he wasn't especially interested in selling Digital Instruments, and he was even less interested in having to deal with, as he put it, "corporate types from back east." In other words, people like me, a born and bred New Yorker who had worked thirty-plus years at Sperry, Litton, Panafax, and now Veeco.

I decided to ignore all the negative feedback and focus only on what we knew about Digital Instruments. When I finally got in to see Virgil, he said he liked the idea of a joint venture between Digital Industries and Veeco, because he'd heard a lot of good things about Veeco's management team. But Virgil was known to be a very shrewd businessman, he could afford to play coy.

Veeco had a plant in Santa Barbara, just a block away from Digital Industries. Every time Jack or I had to go out there, we'd make sure to see Virgil. One or both of us must have visited him at least thirty times over the course of the year. At some point, we lost interest in a joint venture and started talking about a merger. Soon we were actively engaged in a bidding war, and Virgil gleefully watched as the bids increased in large increments. We continued this Kabuki dance for more than two years. In the meantime, Virgil was reevaluating his priorities. He had co-founded a hugely successful company, but success came with a price: personnel problems, quality control issues, missed delivery dates.... The list went on and on, and Elings was a novice in these areas. As the offers got higher and higher, he must have realized he would be a fool not to sell. But the question remained: to whom?

I was convinced that Veeco was the perfect fit for Digital Industries—and vice-versa. Jack and I had spent hours talking to Virgil about our exceptional management team, worldwide distribution network, outstanding service staff, and excellent employee relationships. You name it, we'd bragged about it. Virgil had listened and nodded, but he had on his best poker face.

I dug into my well-worn bag of corporate tricks, hoping to find a sliver of inspiration. One of my favorite poems popped into my head: "The Road Not Taken," by Robert Frost. I couldn't think of a single piece of information about Veeco that Jack or I hadn't already shared with Virgil Elings. We'd bombarded him with facts and figures, but had we addressed his concerns about selling his company to a bunch of "corporate types"? Did he have any idea who we really were when we weren't talking about business? Could he trust us to take care of his company?

I'd been kicking around an answer that seemed either wonderful or ridiculous, depending on my mood. Now, like Frost, I decided to invite Virgil to join me on the road "less traveled," to see where it led us. Virgil was a huge fan of vintage motorcycles, but he also admired classic and rare cars. One afternoon, he showed me beautiful pictures of vintage cars in pristine condition, which sold at auctions for thousands of dollars: a 1966 Ferrari, a 1975 Lamborghini, a 1949 Mercury convertible that reminded me of *Rebel Without a Cause*. Then I read that classic car auctions were held every January in Scottsdale, Arizona. I called Virgil and invited him to meet me there for a long weekend. He could teach me a thing or two about rare cars, and if we had time, we could discuss my plan for merging our two companies.

Virgil asked whether he could invite a couple of friends, and I said, yes, of course. I assumed that they were also physicists or genius inventors, or both. What a surprise to find out that both men were Virgil's high school buddies from Des Moines, Iowa. One was a car salesman, and the other sold building supplies.

I understood then why Virgil was suspicious of corporate types. He was a physics professor, inventor, entrepreneur, and philanthropist, but he'd never lost his connection to his old pals, who had known him long before he became "the" Virgil Elings. That weekend in Scottsdale, he was just one of the guys. We went golfing, we hiked in the mountains, and we scrutinized the cars through Virgil's knowledgeable eye. We tried to outdo one another at dinner with stories that defied belief, and we discovered that we had much more in common than we could have imagined. I flew home knowing that Virgil would make a deal with us. The merger went through in February 1998, and Virgil stayed on as chairman of Digital Instruments for another year.

Digital Instruments enabled Veeco to become the leading designer and manufacturer of scanning probe microscopes. It was one of approximately fifteen acquisitions I facilitated during the 1990s. Our long-range goal was to position Veeco as the primary supplier of equipment to information industries. Jack and I looked at well over a hundred businesses during the decade following our IPO. The companies we bought enabled Veeco to become one of the foremost companies in the fields of data storage, atomic force microscopes, and light-emitting diodes. We developed products that drove a number of key technological innovations. Our processing equipment significantly enabled the development of computers; game boxes such as Nintendo; VCRs, DVRs, and any electronic devices that require mass storage of data. All of these devices needed to store video, audio, photo, and print information in a reliable, easily retrievable manner. Veeco's technology provided the path to faster development of smaller storage devices.

In order to acquire more data storage, we bought Ion Tech, a Colorado-based deposition equipment company, which manufactured a product called DWDM—an enabling filter for the fiber optic industry, and the gateway to the fiber optic technology explosion. This acquisition soon drove Veeco's stock price to more than $105 per share and provided the cash and momentum for additional acquisitions.

Major medical and materials advancements were limited by what the human eye could see. Veeco's atomic force microscope was the tool that was required to make these advances. In our strategic plan for metrology systems, we wanted to be a one-stop shop. We acquired Wyko Corporation, which designed and manufactured optical process metrology systems, because it fit into our concept.

We all knew that LED lighting would revolutionize the computer, television, and lighting industries, but it was slow to enter the marketplace because of its cost. We acquired Emcore Turbodisc, a small company in New Jersey with machines that were essential for manufacturing LEDs. The people at Emcore were years ahead of their time in terms of realizing their potential of LEDs, but they had expended all the capital. They had created a prototype, which we eventually developed into a production machine, making us one of two companies in the world that had that capability. We paid $39 million for the company, and LED products became a billion dollar market by 2011.

When I retired from Veeco in 2006, Ed Braun sent out a letter to all the board members inviting them to attend a special meeting in my honor where he announced that the company had established the Walter J. Scherr Annual Scholarship Program for employees and their children. I felt touched and honored that so many people came from all over the country to say goodbye to me. I loved Veeco with all my heart, but I was ready for the next stage in my life. I looked forward to helping people and in some way paying back what I'd been so fortunate to receive. I felt grateful that I'd participated in the evolution of so much new technology, that I'd been involved in creating a company that continues to help make the world a better place.

In the letter I sent to the company newspaper, my final goodbye to Veeco was this: "The lives we live and the things we do sometimes get in the way of what we wish to say. Today, I give thanks to those who have touched my heart in many ways. May God bless you and grant you health, wealth, wisdom, and peace."

Epilogue

THE DATE WAS JUNE 1938; I WAS AN ALTAR BOY AT OUR LOCAL church, St. Mary Gate of Heaven in Ozone Park, and we were serving mass for a visiting missionary priest from Africa.

The priest spoke with fire and brimstone regarding heaven and hell. We should be preparing ourselves for heaven each day, he thundered.

"How many of you want to go to heaven?" he asked the congregation. Every hand in the audience went up, including mine.

He then smiled and asked the provocative question: "How many of you want to go today?" Not a single hand was raised.

Seventy-four years later and I still don't want to go—not because I am afraid. I have a bucket list that is almost, but not quite, punched out.

One of the last items that I checked off the list is something you read about at the beginning of this book: My visit to the D-Day invasion beaches in Normandy in October 2014. There, I visited the grave of a young soldier from Queens whom I never knew, but who—given our age and proximity—could very well have been me, had things unfolded differently.

At this writing, only two items still remain on my bucket list:

First, I want to develop a program to honor caregivers. I have never forgotten the people who took care of me when I had TB as a young man, or the words of Mother Teresa when I heard her speak in India. I believe that we as a society should not forget those who care for us, in whatever capacity that is. To that end, I am working with the Center for Discovery to develop a "World Cup for Caregivers," a recognition program to honor professional, volunteer, and innovative caregivers around the globe. We hope to launch this program in the New York area in 2016.

Second, I hope to see the expansion of the "iBelieve, iAchieve" program. Sponsored by the Vera and Walter Scherr Foundation, through the auspices of the Family Services of Westchester ARC, this program was initiated in the Yonkers School District in Yonkers, New York a few years ago. The results have been truly inspiring. The objective of iBelieve iAchieve is to match children 4th through 8th grades with positive role models and mentors, and to work collaboratively with schools and community organizations to build a support system that creates incentives to succeed.

To date, almost two dozen children's lives have been positively impacted by the "iBelieve, iAchieve" program. My hope is that this system can be implemented throughout the U.S. I believe, through a partnership of government, higher education, and the corporate community, that we can make this happen, and I hope to be here long enough to see the wheels begin to turn in that direction.

You can learn more about these programs on my website

waltersway.org. And if you feel inspired to help or get involved in these initiatives in any way, we'd be delighted to have your help.

So that's what's left on a nearly 91-year-old man's bucket list; that's what still needs to be accomplished in a life that, has taken me far and wide, on an exhilarating and ultimately satisfying roller coaster ride through the decades.

When these two items are accomplished I can—as we used to say—shuffle off to Buffalo. After all, I've been almost everywhere else!

Acknowledgements

I have had two ventures into "show business" in my life: producing a movie and writing a book. With each endeavor, I underestimated the depth of the workload. I should have anticipated the magnitude of the book project from my experience with making the movie. Nevertheless, it wasn't until I was immersed in the book that I saw the parallels. The effort involved in writing and publishing this book was equivalent to that of producing a movie. I felt a sense of déjà vu! Fortunately, I had a community of family, friends, and colleagues to call on for support. Without the help of what became known as "Team Walter," these pages would have been blank.

Liz Swann was at the starting line when this all began, helping to oversee things from my Sarasota home. She has been with me through completion.

Deborah Chiel, who helped put my thoughts into words on the printed page, brought her creative and professional knowledge. An excellent researcher and gatherer of facts, Deb rarely comes up for air once she's engrossed. She *is* what she's researching, and *Walter's Way* is the better for it.

John Hanc, the author of twelve previous books, brought vast professional knowledge and writing skills. John guided and organized the production process, and along the way he showed me what's involved in creating a book.

Speaking of creative, I want to thank Frank Cusack, the designer of our jacket, who was able to capture the essence of my story with one image.

Roshni Ashar handled the design and typesetting of the text of our book, and we thank her for her cheerful professionalism.

Margaret Tripp Zenk is a copyeditor extraordinaire. *Walter's Way* benefited from her creative ideas and dogged determination.

I'd also like to thank our editor at John Wiley & Sons, Tula Batanchiev; literary agent Linda Konner for helping connect us to Tula and offering other valuable input; and my good friend and adviser on things financial and otherwise, Bill Foster.

Laura Saggese, my beloved daughter, provided invaluable creative input. She also kept her father in check at the most crucial moments. My three sons gave me their loving support and assistance: Bud and Douglas contributed to the chapter on oil exploration. Robert helped me review several key chapters.

Special thanks to the energy pioneers and their wives. As the saying goes, "Behind every great man, there's a great woman." I am grateful to Vera, Maryjane, and Lori for all their years of dedication. They raised their families, made sacrifices, and lent their support to build a successful oil company.

I want to thank my granddaughters: Heather, Karen, Jessica, and Michelle. Their contribution to my Normandy prayer poem was invaluable.

Dr. Ray DeFeo and my sisters Janet Zenk and Helen Fraser critiqued a number of chapters, so my thanks to them.

I'd like to give special shout-out to friends who are really like family. Every year, we share our Scherr family reunion with some of the children of the poker guys you read about in our movie chapter, including Donna and Brad Evans, who helped with the website. What a sight to see: Three festive generations of Scherrs and dear friends celebrating our inspirational love for one another at the wonderful Woodloch Pines Resort in the Pocono Mountains.

The beneficiary of this book is The Center for Discovery. I have benefited by working with some terrific people from The Center, and my thanks to them for their wonderful assistance on this book: Bill Evans, Steve Mosenson, Richard Humleker, and Patrick Dollard and his merry legion of angels. Their philosophy celebrates each individual's abilities rather than disabilities.

A special thanks to Dr. George Todd, who introduced me to The Center for Discovery, which certainly changed my outlook on life, if not my life itself.

You've read in this book about my devotion to my beloved wife Vera. In 2003, after a three-year battle with illness, she died quietly in the Northport home that she filled with such love for her family. She is not gone, however. She is with me, and I know how proud she would be of this endeavor.

I also want to express my appreciation to my children, grandchildren, and great-grandchildren for their support and love: Douglas, Lori, Jessica, Cory, Alyssa, Haven, and Gianna; Bud, Maryjane, Heather,

Karen, John (Walter IV), and Erin; Laura, Ed, Michelle, Michael and Matthew; and Robert, Marisol, Jonathan, and Christian.

I am truly fortunate to have married a second time. My wife Sylvia is a very loving and wonderful woman, who enthusiastically supported this project. She contributed many invaluable insights that added greatly to the book.

I have one wish for you, the reader: that you, too, could have the experience of writing your life story. I believe that in doing so, you would see that a guiding light determines your purpose in life. In Normandy, I wiped the special sand over the name of the solder on the cross, which made it bright and clear. Writing a book would do the same for you.

Why, God, Not Me?
By Walter Scherr

A bucket list is mandatory when you get to be my age,

To finish things so long put off so I can turn the page.

I took my time, I wrote my list, peace I hoped to find,

So I can leave this place called Earth with a clearer mind.

Atop my list at number one was a visit to the beaches of D-Day,

To pay my respects to the young heroes who bravely led the way.

To understand at last, dear God, why it was not me,

Who died beneath those tall white cliffs that day in Normandy.

I stepped up and volunteered to fight, for our country dear,

But tests revealed I had active TB, so they said I must stay here.

If I was healthy, I well know, it could have been me who fell that day,

Instead of my neighbor, Francis Bowen, who was lost among the fray.

These many years I've carved a path to match his sacrifice,

So that I did not regret the life I lead or how I rolled the dice.

To understand at last, dear God, why it was not me,

Who died beneath those tall white cliffs that day in Normandy.

The final chapter of my life is coming to a close,

As time passes, day by day, life around me slows.

I made the trip, I felt the rain, I prayed there at his grave,

I honored Francis Bowen and the other men so brave.

And as I knelt there, deep in prayer, it all became quite clear,

God blesses me, and Francis, and all the other heroes who lay near.

And I understood at last, dear God, why it was not me,

Who died beneath those tall white cliffs that day in Normandy.